zyrtec 150     2x> /day

The Environmental Vision of Thomas Merton

# Culture of the Land: A Series in the New Agrarianism

This series is devoted to the exploration and articulation of a new agrarianism that considers the health of habitats and human communities together. It demonstrates how agrarian insights and responsibilities can be worked out in diverse fields of learning and living: history, science, art, politics, economics, literature, philosophy, religion, urban planning, education, and public policy. Agrarianism is a comprehensive worldview that appreciates the intimate and practical connections that exist between humans and the earth. It stands as our most promising alternative to the unsustainable and destructive ways of current global, industrial, and consumer culture.

## Series Editor
Norman Wirzba, Duke University, North Carolina

## Advisory Board
Wendell Berry, Port Royal, Kentucky
Ellen Davis, Duke University, North Carolina
Patrick Holden, Soil Association, United Kingdom
Wes Jackson, Land Institute, Kansas
Gene Logsdon, Upper Sandusky, Ohio
Bill McKibben, Middlebury College, Vermont
David Orr, Oberlin College, Ohio
Michael Pollan, University of California at Berkeley, California
Jennifer Sahn, *Orion* Magazine, Massachusetts
Vandana Shiva, Research Foundation for Science,
Technology, and Ecology, India
Bill Vitek, Clarkson University, New York

# The Environmental Vision of Thomas Merton

Monica Weis, SSJ

THE UNIVERSITY PRESS OF KENTUCKY

Scholarly publisher for the Commonwealth,
serving Bellarmine University, Berea College, Centre
College of Kentucky, Eastern Kentucky University,
The Filson Historical Society, Georgetown College,
Kentucky Historical Society, Kentucky State University,
Morehead State University, Murray State University,
Northern Kentucky University, Transylvania University,
University of Kentucky, University of Louisville,
and Western Kentucky University.
All rights reserved.

Unless otherwise stated, all photographs are reproduced courtesy of
the Thomas Merton Center at Bellarmine University.

*Editorial and Sales Offices:* The University Press of Kentucky
663 South Limestone Street, Lexington, Kentucky 40508-4008
www.kentuckypress.com

15 14 13 12 11      5 4 3 2 1

Library of Congress Cataloging-in-Publication Data

Weis, Monica, 1942–
  The environmental vision of Thomas Merton / Monica Weis.
    p.    cm. — (Culture of the land)
  Includes bibliographical references and index.
  ISBN 978-0-8131-3004-0 (hardcover : alk. paper) —
  ISBN 978-0-8131-3015-6 (ebook)
  1. Merton, Thomas, 1915–1968. 2. Nature—Religious aspects—Catholic
Church. I. Title.
  BX1795.N36W45 2011
  261.8'8092—dc22
                                        2011001508

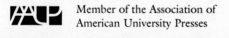

For the fourteen founders of the
International Thomas Merton Society,
who continue to inspire me to delve into
the richness of Thomas Merton's life and writing.
May they be blessed abundantly.

# Contents

# Illustrations

# Foreword

"*Caeli enarrant gloriam Dei*": "The heavens proclaim the glory of God; and the firmament shows forth His handiwork" (Psalm 19:1). Thomas Merton chanted these words from the psalms almost every week for the twenty-seven years of his monastic life. These, along with many other expressions found in the psalms, served to deepen Merton's awareness of creation as a manifestation of God in the world. Long before he entered the monastery, however, Merton showed a profound perception of creation and its message to all who are attuned. In this book Monica Weis shows us something of Merton's own inner life in relation to creation and how this developed beginning early in his life. She does this in such a way as to demonstrate that this is important not only for Merton and his own development, but for each one of us as we likewise strive to take part in the dance of creation.

Merton shows that it will be impossible to take part in this dance so long as we view creation and other people simply as objects; doing so removes the seer from direct contact with the reality he or she sees. Merton illustrates this by contrasting the way a child views a tree—a vision "which is utterly simple, uncolored by prejudice, and 'new'"—with the lumberman's vision "entirely conditioned by profit motives and considerations of business." He says that "this *exaggeration of* the subject-object relationship by material interest and technical speculation is one of the main obstacles to contemplation" (IE 20–21). This reveals the extent to which his love and appreciation of nature and creation are a profound part of his own contemplative experience.

In her introduction Weis highlights three pivotal moments in Merton's life. The first, in the late 1950s, was his experience at Fourth and Walnut in Louisville, where he suddenly realized that "I loved all people and that they are a part of me." The second, in 1963, was the experience that triggered his letter to Rachel Carson, an experience of his oneness with all of nature. The third, in 1968, was the experience at the Buddha statues in Ceylon, where he was drawn into oneness with all that is. Each of these events serves as an indication of what Merton calls "the need to clear away the clouds of self-deception which we cast over external reality when we set ourselves to thinking about it." We are called not to "think about" reality, but to enter into it in the depth of our experience, knowing that what we encounter is ultimately the Voice of God.

When Jesus spoke in the Sermon on the Mount about how the heavenly Father cares for the birds of the air, the flowers of the field, and the grass of the ground, he was giving us more than simply a lesson in God's Providence. He was ultimately telling us how the birds of the air and flowers of the field are a manifestation of God to us. Likewise, when he used parables to teach, he was telling us how every element of creation is a revelation of God and of his Love for every person and every being. Like the Zen master, he was trying to lead us to "that direct, immediate view in which the experience of a subject-object duality is destroyed."

Similarly, one might interpret original sin in Genesis as the very sin that brought this subject-object duality into the world. When God created Adam and Eve, he said: "Be fruitful and multiply, and fill the earth; and have dominion over the birds of the air and over every living thing that moves upon the earth. . . . And God saw everything that He had made, and behold it was very good" (Genesis 1:29–31). It was all "very good" because now Adam and Eve, along with all living creatures, were to be a perfect reflection and manifestation of God within the world. They were to join together in the great dance of creation before God. But by original sin, Adam and Eve ate of the tree of good and evil. They introduced the element of duality into the world. They viewed the fruit of the tree not as a manifestation of the goodness of

God, but as an object that could make them "like unto God." They failed to recognize that they were already created not only "like unto God," but in the very image and likeness of God within the world. In this way they no longer entered into the dance of creation, but had to hide from God "because they were naked."

In this book Monica Weis shows us how Thomas Merton experienced that "direct, immediate view" of creation, as well as the effect this had on his own contemplative life, and that contemplative life to which he felt all people are called. The book is very timely for several reasons: first, because today people everywhere are becoming more aware of the importance of ecology for the future of our planet. Merton would caution, however, that conservation of our environment does not go far enough by itself. It is not sufficient simply to "preserve" nature and creation. The ultimate meaning of creation, and hence of ecology, can be found only in the mystery of the Incarnation. For when God became man, he took to himself not only human flesh and nature, but all of creation. He reestablished the oneness between God and creation and reordered the dance of creation. Hence, when we look at creation, it cannot be simply an esthetic experience, but one that leads directly to a contemplative experience and even a mystical one.

In *New Seeds of Contemplation,* Merton says: "If we believe in the Incarnation of the Son of God, there is no one on earth in whom we are not prepared to see, in mystery, the presence of Christ" (NSC 296). The same can ultimately be said of all creation. It was this awareness that gradually increased throughout Merton's life, and which should increase in every person's life. As Weis shows, Merton's increasing awareness manifested itself in his writing, both prose and poetry, which may indicate that the poet is actually more closely in touch with reality than the person who sees only the external reality.

Another reason for this book's timeliness lies in the fact that, as I write, our nation is facing the most serious man-made catastrophe of our history, in the tragic oil spill in the Gulf of Mexico. This event, along with the decisions that led up to it, shows the contrast between two responses to creation that Merton indicated: whether we approach creation with the simple awe and reverence of the child or with the greed and grasping of the lumberjack or oilman. Currently we do not see "the dance of the raven," but rather the immobility of the oil-coated pelican. This is because, like Adam and Eve, we have tried to control creation out of our own selfish greed and have failed to approach it with the reverence and awe that is due to it as a manifestation of God.

Thomas Merton can show us the way to return to the original stance regarding creation. Monica Weis can help us discover not only Merton's approach to creation and the way that it led him to God, but the way that we can imitate him in this pursuit. Merton gives us a set of tools that can be used for this conversion of heart. His grasp of creation as a gift of God can be found in his prose, his poetry, his photography, his journaling, and his love and friendship with many other people. If we were to apply these same tools in our own lives, perhaps we could begin to discover anew that dance of creation. That dance already goes on in the depths of our hearts. Saint Paul tells us: "Creation waits with eager longing for the revealing of the children of God; because the creation itself will be set free from its bondage to decay and obtain the glorious liberty of the children of God. We know that the whole creation has been groaning in travail together until now; and not only the creation, but we ourselves, who have the first fruits of the Spirit, groan inwardly as we wait for adoption as children. For in this hope we were saved" (Romans 8:19–24).

Fr. James Conner, OCSO
Abbey of Gethsemani

# Acknowledgments

It is often said that we stand on the shoulders of those who have gone before us. This wisdom applies in particular to the genesis of this book. There are many shoulders upon which I stand. Some years ago William H. Shannon nudged me to explore the ways in which nature influenced Thomas Merton; not long after that, in a talk at Nazareth College, Lawrence Cunningham suggested that there was a book to be written about Merton and nature. An NEH Institute award during the summer of 1997 solidified my thinking. Collegial support from Patrick O'Connell, Jonathan Montaldo, and Bonnie Thurston continued to challenge me to stretch toward this goal. I am grateful to these Merton scholars for their confidence that I had something to contribute to the ongoing dialogue exploring the depths of Merton's thinking and spirituality. To Brother Patrick Hart, Anne McCormick and the Merton Legacy Trust, my gratitude for their quiet encouragement, and to Brother James Conner for his gracious foreword. Special kudos to Christine Bochen for her friendship and willingness to read an early draft of this book and help me untangle its organizational problems. To Paul Pearson, grateful acknowledgment of his comprehensive view of the Merton Archives and suggestions for my research that have made this a stronger book. Sincere thanks to Jennifer Burr, Nazareth College reference librarian, who graciously discovered elusive references. A hug of appreciation to Corynn O'Connor and Elana Augustine, who painstakingly checked the accuracy of quotations. And, of course, long-term gratitude goes to my religious community, the Sisters of St.

Joseph of Rochester, who provided both physical and psychological space for the writing of this book. My thanks also to Nazareth College for a summer 2010 grant that has helped underwrite permissions for the photos in this book.

Several of the chapters that follow contain material previously published as lectures or articles; they have been substantially rethought and expanded for this study. I acknowledge permission to quote from some of my earlier publications.

"Beyond the Shadow and the Disguise: 'Spots of Time' in Thomas Merton's Spiritual Development." *The Merton Seasonal* 23.1 (Spring 1998): 21–27.

"The Birds Ask: 'Is It Time to Be?': Thomas Merton's Moments of Spiritual Awakening." In *Beyond the Shadow and the Disguise: Three Essays on Thomas Merton*, edited by Keith Griffin, 10–27. Holmfirth, West Yorkshire: Thomas Merton Society of Great Britain and Ireland, 2006.

"Dancing with the Raven: Thomas Merton's Evolving View of Nature." In *The Vision of Thomas Merton*, edited by Patrick F. O'Connell, 135–53. Notre Dame: Ave Maria Press, 2003.

"Dwelling in Eden: Thomas Merton's Return to Paradise." In *Riscritture dell'Eden*, edited by Andrea Mariani, 225–44. Rome: Liguori Editore, 2005.

"Kindred Spirits in Revelation and Revolution: Rachel Carson and Thomas Merton." *The Merton Annual* 19 (2006): 128–41.

"Living Beings Call Us to Reflective Living: Mary Austin, Thomas Merton, and Contemporary Nature Writers." *The Merton Seasonal* 17.4 (Autumn 1992): 4–9.

"Merton's Fascination with Deer: A Graceful Symphony." *The Merton Journal: Journal of the Thomas Merton Society of Great Britain & Ireland* 15.2 (Advent 2008): 33–46.

"Rambling with the Early Merton." *The Merton Seasonal* 28.2 (Summer 2003): 3–6.

*Thomas Merton's Gethsemani: Landscapes of Paradise*. Lexington: University Press of Kentucky, 2005.

"The Wilderness of Compassion: Nature's Influence on Thomas Merton." *The Merton Annual* 14 (2001): 56–80.

# Abbreviations

| | |
|---|---|
| AJ | *The Asian Journal* |
| CGB | *Conjectures of a Guilty Bystander* |
| CP | *Collected Poems of Thomas Merton* |
| CT | *The Courage for Truth* |
| CWA | *Contemplation in a World of Action* |
| DS | *Day of a Stranger* |
| DWL | *Dancing in the Water of Life* |
| ES | *Entering the Silence* |
| IE | *The Inner Experience* |
| LL | *Learning to Love* |
| NSC | *New Seeds of Contemplation* |
| OSM | *The Other Side of the Mountain* |
| PAJ | *Preview of the Asian Journey* |
| RJ | *The Road to Joy* |
| RM | *Run to the Mountain* |
| RU | *Raids on the Unspeakable* |
| SC | *Seeds of Contemplation* |
| SJ | *The Sign of Jonas* |
| SS | *A Search for Solitude* |
| SSM | *The Seven Storey Mountain* |
| TB | *Tom's Book* |
| TS | *Thoughts in Solitude* |
| TTW | *Turning toward the World* |
| VW | *A Vow of Conversation* |
| WF | *Witness to Freedom* |
| ZBA | *Zen and the Birds of Appetite* |

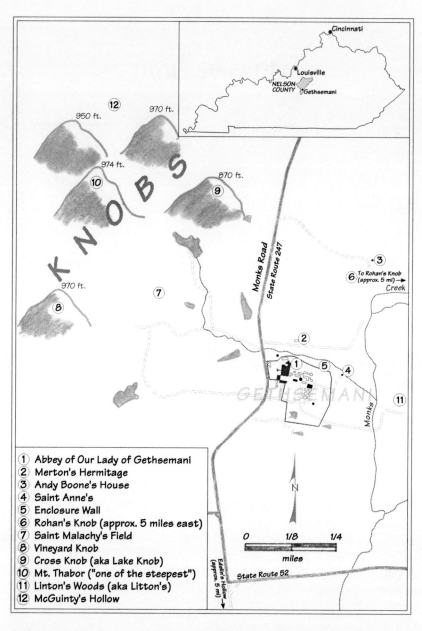

Legend:
1. Abbey of Our Lady of Gethsemani
2. Merton's Hermitage
3. Andy Boone's House
4. Saint Anne's
5. Enclosure Wall
6. Rohan's Knob (approx. 5 miles east)
7. Saint Malachy's Field
8. Vineyard Knob
9. Cross Knob (aka Lake Knob)
10. Mt. Thabor ("one of the steepest")
11. Linton's Woods (aka Litton's)
12. McGuinty's Hollow

Gethsemani, our place in creation. (Dick Gilbreath, University of Kentucky Cartography Lab)

# Introduction
## Dancing with the Raven

Nature was always important in Thomas Merton's life—from his infancy in Prades, France, when he learned words like chrysanthemum, hollyhock, foxglove, chickadee, and kingfisher from his mother's careful coaching, to long hours in the fresh air watching his artist father create landscapes, to his final years of solitude in the hermitage at Our Lady of Gethsemani, the Trappist monastery in Kentucky. In all these places Merton was intrigued by nature and allowed it to shape his spirituality and consciousness.

In contemporary society, attention to nature—its beauty, its integrity, and our interdependence with it—is a fairly common concept. Indeed, numerous organizations and Web sites are devoted to conservation of specific species, particular bioregions, and wide-ranging principles of responsible stewardship. In the early 1960s, however, when Thomas Merton was becoming more aware of environmental responsibility, such consciousness was not trendy. Although ecological thinking in some rudimentary form can be traced to ancient Greek times, the concept of ecology surfaced in Western culture in the eighteenth and nineteenth centuries in the writings of men such as Alexander von Humboldt, Alfred Russel Wallace, Karl Möbius, and Charles Darwin. The word *ecology* (*oikos* = household and *logos* = knowledge) was first used by the German biologist Ernst Haeckel in 1866 to mean the study of an organism in relationship to its environment; shortly thereafter, ecology became a distinct discipline through Eugen Warming's research on biotic communities. It was not until the twentieth century, however, that the concept of ecology was extended to the social sciences and the humanities, and not until the second half of that century did "delphic voices" of best-selling nature writers give birth to the "Age of Ecology" and what the intellectual historian Donald Worster has identified as multiple views of the "economy of nature."[1] And it was not until 1972 that the United Nations began its "Think Globally, Act Locally" campaign, a few years before the rise in popularity of James Lovelock's Gaia hypothesis, which viewed the planet as a living organism of interdependent species and elements.

But in the 1960s Americans were more concerned with the domestic conflict over the Vietnam War and nuclear proliferation; tension about civil rights for blacks; the first stirrings of justice for indigenous people; initial suspicion of the dangers of technology; and incipient awareness of the positive effect of nonviolence. Thomas Merton, although a monk vowed to prayer and silence, was in the forefront of dialogue on these social issues, writing essays for *Jubilee, Ramparts,* the *Center,* the *Catholic Worker,* and any journal that would publish his voice in the wilderness—so much so that the Trappist order forbade him to comment publicly on war. True to his contemplative spirit and commitment to truth, Merton found a way around this censure between October 1961 and October 1962 by periodically sending a collection of mimeographed letters about the illogic and immorality of war to a circle of friends—recently published as *Cold War Letters.*[2]

Nevertheless, Merton's vision for wholeness and his awareness of the challenges to contemporary living were not confined to aspects of *human* justice. His lifelong interaction with nature continued feeding his spirituality and broadening the scope of his concern. Indeed, his last few publications before his untimely death in Bangkok, Thailand, on December 10, 1968, indicate that issues of *environmental* justice were frequently on Merton's mind. Well before any United Nations declaration or new paradigm of our solar system based on astronauts' view from outer space in 1972, Merton was sensing our responsibility for the environmental health of this planet. If I were to identify a single moment that reveals Merton's movement toward greater responsibility for nature, it would be his January 12, 1963, letter to Rachel Carson (WF 70–72). After reading her seminal book, *Silent Spring,* Merton was so touched by Carson' s insight into what she offered as "evidence for the diagnosis of the ills of our civilization" that he responded to her with a heartfelt letter that must be considered a watershed moment in his spiritual growth. Such a transformative moment is akin to his Fourth and Walnut experience, when he realized that he could not sequester himself from humanity in a monastery precisely because he was related to all these people who were "shining like the sun" (CGB 157). Such a transformative moment is similar also to Merton's encounter with the huge reclining Buddhas at Polonnaruwa, Ceylon, when he knew and felt in the depths of his being that he was now seeing "beyond the shadow and the disguise" (AJ 233–35).

Incisive and decisive moments such as these are often referred to by psychologists and spiritual directors as touchstone moments: significant times when a deep and permanent insight takes root in a person's understanding. Such monumental events then become yardsticks by which to measure the validity of subsequent experience; they become memories to return to for solace and wisdom when facing new challenges and decisions; they are *kairos* moments in human development that chronicle important and irreversible flashes of vision or spurts of spiritual growth. William Wordsworth, the British Romantic poet, called such experiences "spots of time"—a conflation of where and when something important occurs. In book 12 of his autobiographical poem, *The Prelude: The Growth of the Poet's Mind,* Wordsworth describes these "spots of time" as moments of healing by which "our minds / Are nourished and invisibly repaired"—a deeply felt experience that "enables us to mount, / When high, more high, and lifts us up when fallen."[3]

*The Environmental Vision of Thomas Merton,* which explores the powerful influence of nature on Thomas Merton's spiritual development and budding ecological consciousness, is not intended to repeat the comprehensive biographical facts and wonderful insights of Merton scholars such as Michael Mott and William H. Shannon. It does, however, hold up to the light several "spots of time" that, in

*Book Focus*

this writer's opinion, offer testimony as to where and when Thomas Merton's spiritual journey moved from mere delight in nature to a committed responsibility for its welfare—a movement that places Merton ahead of his time in environmental thinking and unique in his approach to our relationship with nature. This book invites Merton readers to stretch their thinking about the spiritual and social concerns of this writer-monk and encourages environmentalists to take another look at this prophetic voice from the mid-twentieth century. Key to Thomas Merton's transformation toward an ecological consciousness is the act of *seeing*—that is, seeing more deeply and comprehensively, being awake to one's surroundings at a soul-stirring level, by which one is—in Wordsworth's words—"nourished and invisibly repaired."

Going beyond mere looking to really *seeing* and becoming awake is a central concept in American nature writing, in Christianity, and, indeed, in all major religious traditions. Henry David Thoreau cast himself as chanticleer calling his neighbors to awake (*Walden*); Walt Whitman would have us ignore the astronomer with his numbers and theories in favor of gazing on the awesome night sky (*Leaves of Grass*). Jesus admonished his disciples to "stay awake! For you do not know when the Son of Man will come" (Matthew 24:42). The Buddha or bodhi is the one who is awake; the Sufi poet Rumi was fond of calling Muslims to wake up, to experience the realization that prayer is better than sleep.

Thomas Merton, too, was no stranger to the importance of *seeing* and the power of becoming *awake*. Many times in his writings Merton challenges us to be on the alert, to see more deeply into our experience. His own commitment to rising at 2:15 A.M. was driven not only by his monastic *horarium*, but also by his need to be present for the first hint of sunrise—to be awake at the creation of a new day. In *Day of a Stranger*, a description of his life in the hermitage, Merton celebrates this dawn ritual by reciting the psalms of Vigils and Lauds that "grow up silently by themselves without effort like plants in this light which is favorable to them" (DS 43). Merton's personal experience, monastic practice, and fruits of prayer made his approach to nature and ecological issues unique. Indeed, in *New Seeds of Contemplation*,

Introduction

Merton offers us a definition of contemplation that challenges all human beings—not just vowed contemplatives—to become more awake.
Contemplation, he writes, is "life itself, fully awake, fully alive, fully
aware that it is alive. . . . It is spontaneous awe at the sacredness of life,
of being" (NSC 1).

*The Environmental Vision of Thomas Merton* examines Merton's
commitment to seeing and increased awareness and explores some of
the consequences of that commitment: his deepening sense of place
and desire for solitude; his expanded love and responsibility for human and nonhuman life; and his evolving ecological consciousness.
Chapter 1 offers an analysis of Merton's letter to Rachel Carson and
a brief clarification of how these two literary minds were prophets of
both revelation and revolution. Merton's January 12, 1963, letter is a
watershed moment, or "spot of time," in his developing environmental consciousness. Chapter 2 focuses on Merton's gift of awareness and
sense of place—from his infant days in Prades, France, to his entrance
into the Trappist monastery in Kentucky and the turning point of June
27, 1949, when the abbot permitted Merton to pray beyond the confines of the monastery cloister. Chapter 3 applies the concept of "spots
of time" to three graced moments that reveal Merton's increasing reliance on nature for his spiritual growth: his impetuous climb up a Kentucky knob on New Year's Day 1950; his encounter with a hawk on
February 10, 1950; and his meditation in the 1960s on the awakening
of the birds at *le point vierge* of the day.

Chapter 4—central to the book—examines passages from Merton's journals, spanning several years, to offer ongoing evidence of
the multiple ways nature and ordinary experiences influenced his writing, thinking, and praying. Noting the increasing frequency of such
passages reveals how nature images function in several specific ways:
focusing his poetic eye, thinking in metaphors, and reporting on the
weather. Chapter 5 concentrates on Merton's inner and outer landscapes, investigating how love of nature overflowed into prayer; how
prayer often expanded into celebration of nature; and how frequently,
in his years of more intense solitude, inner and outer landscapes intertwined and merged into a new awareness that underpinned his poetry

and his fascination with photography, and which prepared Merton for discovering his responsibility for justice for creation. Chapter 6 traces the steps of this emerging ecological consciousness—from his letter to Rachel Carson in 1963 until his last published book review a few months before his death in 1968. The assortment of letters, journal entries, reading notebooks, and published book reviews written during these five years reveals Merton on the cutting edge of environmental thinking and developing what Aldo Leopold—and later Merton—called an ecological conscience. A brief afterword offers a vignette or snapshot of Merton's spiritual journey—his story in miniature—as he learned to interact responsibly with the deer in the woods surrounding his hermitage.

 *Seeing* and becoming aware, developing both a sense of place and an ecological consciousness, are important concepts in this study of Merton's spirituality, but I would like to digress briefly to explore the title of this introduction. Robert E. Daggy, in his introduction to volume 5 of Merton's journals—*Dancing in the Water of Life*—suggests that the raven, with its double symbolism of blessing and mischief making, is an apt image for the paradoxical Merton. Daggy views Merton in these years as dancing a quadrille of indecision—opting for the hermitage, yet grasping on to the momentary gratification of friends (DWL xii). I find the image of the raven—and the phrase "dancing with the raven"—fruitful for thinking about the paradoxical Merton. Even though Merton's journals reveal that he did not much care for crows because of their quarrelsome and vociferous nature, he nevertheless made peace with these noisy birds in the woods near the hermitage, and he even copied into a 1964 Reading Notebook a Charles Lear limerick about a raven (DWL xi). Who is this mysterious bird?

Old World literature associates the raven with pestilence, battle, and death. Anglo-Saxon poems such as *Judith* and *Beowulf* celebrate ravens waiting to devour the dead. In several plays of Shakespeare ravens are associated with sinners. In Zen mythology the raven—because it feeds on carrion—is regarded as a bird of insatiable appetite. Merton acknowledges this symbolism in his *Zen and the Birds of Appetite* (1968). Biblical literature also names the raven as omen, both good and bad. The prophet Isaiah (34:11), for example, reminds us that ravens descended on the lands of the wicked; in Proverbs 30:17 these birds pluck out the eyes of sinners. Jewish tradition teaches that because the raven—the first bird Noah sent on a reconnaissance mission from the ark—did not return, its feathers were blackened, and its diet restricted to carrion. Greek mythology, on the other hand, believes the raven's colorful feathers were turned black because of unfaithfulness to a lover.

Yet ravens can also be guardians and bearers of blessing. Ravens were sent to feed Elijah during the long drought (1 Kings 17:6), and they symbolize divine Providence in the Psalms (147:9) and the book of Job (38:41). In the Song of Solomon (also called the Song of Songs), the Beloved's locks are "black as a raven" (5:11). In Christian iconography, the raven can symbolize solitude and is often depicted accompanying Abbot Anthony in the desert and Saint Paul the Hermit, and the bird becomes the special protector of Saint Benedict, the founder of Western monasticism.

Many indigenous cultures regard the raven as a shape-shifter, an omen of impending evil or death. This view continues today in modern magic, witchcraft, and mystery, yet ravens, according to the biologist Bernd Heinrich, are also regarded as the "brains" of the bird world.[4] Early Celtic lore claimed that the raven was a symbol of second sight. Pacific Northwest tribes regard the raven as a hero, messenger, and sign of maternal care and spiritual strength, as well as a trickster and creator of the world. Some people regard the raven as a god, "one who speaks with strong words." The well-known anthropologist Richard Nelson notes that to the Koyukon people in the Arctic, the raven is not first and foremost a bird, but "a person and a power, God in a clown's suit, incarnation of a once-omnipotent spirit. Raven sees, hears, understands, reveals . . . determines."[5] The Haida people, also in the Pacific Northwest, revere Raven as the one who stole light from the sacred box and scattered it through the sky to become the night stars and the one bright light of day. Using his seductive voice, Raven then lured the first humans from a clamshell, mated them with chitons (primitive mollusks), and created the first generation of the Haida. In Tsimshian oral literature, this "origin story" is transformed into a "culture hero story." Raven, disguised as a baby, plays with his grandfather's box containing the sunlight, reassumes his shape, flies off to a group of fisherman he has befriended, and sets the sun free.

However we regard the raven—as blessing or trickster, as having positive or negative import—Robert Daggy is astute in suggesting the bird as a workable symbol for Thomas Merton, especially in its role as "one who speaks strong words." Merton's need to speak out on social issues yet drink deeply from the waters of contemplation, and his passion to interact with others whom he saw "shining like the sun" yet withdraw into the solitude of the hermitage, make the raven an appropriate image for this writer-monk, contemplative-activist, this man of many faces, this man of compassion and passion for the world of humans and nonhumans. The image of dancing with the raven would, I believe, delight Merton's sense of humor and his keenness to have us join him in the general dance of life.

All pertinent quotes from Merton's writing could in no way be included in this text. There are just too many. I hope, however, that the references chosen will pique your interest to delve more deeply into Merton's writing and spiritual thinking. There are books yet to be written about Merton's study of *theoria physica* and his commitment to the woods; biblical wilderness and paradise consciousness; the ability of nature to evoke memory; Merton's vow of stability and the power of place. These ideas are just the tip of the iceberg. It is my hope that this initial study of Merton's interaction with nature and evolution of an ecological consciousness will invite scholarly dialogue and ongoing research from Merton scholars and ecocritics into this little-known yet important aspect of Merton's life.

# Chapter 1

# Encountering Rachel Carson
## Environmentalist and Provocateur

> I love the nature that is all around me here. And I regret my
> own follies with DDT, which I have now totally renounced.
> —Thomas Merton to Rachel Carson

January 1963: the United States was celebrating the six-month anniversary of the opening of its first Walmart superstore, yet still grieving the August 1962 death of Marilyn Monroe. The first black student registered at the University of Mississippi was beginning his second semester of study, and the Cuban missile crisis of October continued to be debated in smoke-filled men's clubs. George Wallace was inaugurated as governor of Alabama, defiantly proclaiming, "Segregation now, segregation tomorrow, and segregation forever!" The singer Patsy Cline had only a few weeks to live before her tragic death in a plane crash. The first disco had opened in Los Angeles, and Beatlemania was just beginning to gather momentum in the United States. Martin Luther King Jr. had not yet given his "I Have a Dream" speech, and John F. Kennedy was still president—at least for eleven more months. On January 12 Thomas Merton felt compelled to write a letter to Rachel Carson, author of the recently published *Silent Spring*.

Though January 1963 itself was a somewhat quiet month, January 12 marked a turning point in the ecological consciousness of Thomas Merton—a day of revelation and revolution, when a significant spiritual insight effected a dramatic and permanent change in his attitude

and behavior. Indeed, Merton's reading of *Silent Spring* was an epiphanic event akin to other well-known and powerful moments of spiritual insight in his life. One thinks immediately of Merton's experience
at Fourth and Walnut streets in Louisville, Kentucky, when he realized
how intimately he was connected to every other human being; or those
years in the late 1950s and early 1960s, termed by scholars his "turning toward the world," when, as the fruit of prayer, Merton became increasingly aware of how closely social justice was linked to his monastic
vocation of silence and solitude. Merton had been intimately involved
in the antiwar movement and, despite being silenced by his Trappist
superiors, was still sending a collection of his mimeographed "Cold
War letters" to friends and acquaintances. But his insatiable appetite
for new ideas and horizons of thought propelled him to latch on to the
growing hot topic of 1963: the evils of DDT. One might characterize
this event by paraphrasing Robert Frost: two roads *converged* in a yellow wood . . . and that has made all the difference. Two writers, two
lives, one heart. Let's set the scene.

Since 1939 DDT had been used successfully to eradicate mosquito
larvae; during World War II the American military lavishly sprayed the
Pacific Islands with this chemical before an invasion. When malaria was
significantly reduced in developed countries, Paul Müller was awarded
a Nobel Prize for his discovery of DDT's insecticidal qualities. By the
mid-1950s most U.S. municipalities were spraying DDT in neighbor-
hoods to eradicate tent caterpillars, gypsy moths, and the beetles responsible for Dutch elm disease.[1] Yet all was not well. Rachel Carson,
working as an information specialist for the U.S. Fish and Wildlife Service, had in 1945 submitted an article to *Reader's Digest* detailing the
disruptive influence of DDT on the delicate balance of nature. Despite
the fact that she had been an occasional contributor to the magazine
for almost ten years and had once sought a position as its science editor, her article was not accepted. As Carson's biographer Linda Lear
comments, "The *Digest* . . . found pesticides an unpalatable subject,
and Rachel turned her attention to other research subjects."[2]

Now in the early 1960s, when a friend in Massachusetts asked
why all the songbirds in her yard had died along with the mosquitoes,

Carson was persuaded to tackle this question. *Silent Spring,* published in three installments in the *New Yorker* magazine beginning in June 1962 and in a single volume by Houghton Mifflin that September, called for a major paradigm shift in our thinking—a bold proposal for a postwar America where "science was god, and science was male."[3] All hell broke loose. Negative comments from scientists, politicians, and chemical company executives—a veritable international controversy—threatened to destroy her. Carson's writing and scientific career seemed to be at an end. Targeted in a vicious and financially underwritten campaign to discredit her scientific integrity, Carson was vilified as a "hysterical female," a "pseudo-scientist," "probably a communist," a "bird and bunny lover," and a charlatan researcher.[4]

The controversy over *Silent Spring*—what former Vice President Al Gore has termed the "power of an idea" against the "power of politicians"[5]—fueled public debate, and "people began to think about the chemicals they were handling, what they were doing to the environment, and what scientists weren't telling them. . . . They began to question the very direction of technology."[6] Rachel Carson—the mouse that roared—was heard.

Nearly fifty years later, we can verify that *Silent Spring* became the catalyst for our current environmental movement. Carson's "third eye" allowed her to see beneath the surface to a new truth about nature, namely, the interdependence of all creation: soil, air, water, animals, and human beings. As Lear notes, "From childhood on, Carson was interested in the long history of the earth, in its patterns and rhythms, its ancient seas, its evolving life forms. She was an ecologist—fascinated by intersections and connections but always aware of the whole—before that perspective was accorded scholarly legitimacy." Moreover, she witnessed firsthand her town of Springdale, Pennsylvania, succumb to chemical emissions and industrial waste as neighboring Pittsburgh rose to prominence in the iron and steel industry.[7]

Before 1962 the word environment was not a public-policy term; two years earlier, conservation matters had been mentioned only peripherally at both the Democratic and Republican conventions.[8] But concern over nuclear fallout, the pesticide-contaminated cranberry scandal of 1959, and widespread infant deformities in Europe that were due to the drug thalidomide had created public readiness for a new message. Carson's meticulous research, combined with her lyrical explanation of the dangers of pesticides, not only put the issue of pesticides into the public debate, but directly led to the establishment of the Environmental Protection Agency in 1970 and a ban on the production of DDT in 1972. Widely regarded as the most influential book in the last fifty years, *Silent Spring* is credited by Thomas J. Lyon and Al Gore, among others, with inaugurating a new era of environmental concern, a watershed moment of new vision and activism.[9] In 1980, presenting Rachel Carson posthumously with the Presidential Medal of Freedom, President Jimmy Carter said, "She created a tide of environmental consciousness that has not ebbed."[10] More recently, the historian Gary Kroll has claimed that *Silent Spring* was "so much more than an anti-pesticide tract. It was an essay of ecological radicalism that attempted to wake up a populace quiescent to the techo-scientific control of the world."[11]

Late in 1962 Thomas Merton became aware of Carson's book and, even before reading it, confided in his journal:

> I have been shocked at a notice of a new book, by Rachel Carson [*Silent Spring*], on what is happening to birds as a result of the indiscriminate use of poisons (which do not manage to kill all the insects they intend to kill). Someone will say: you worry about birds: why not worry about people? I worry about *both* birds and people. We are in the world and part of it and we are destroying everything because we are destroying ourselves, spiritually, morally and in every way. It is all part of the same sickness, and it all hangs together. (TTW 274)

Through the efforts of Anne Ford, a friend of his at Houghton Mifflin, Merton secured a copy of *Silent Spring* shortly after it hit the bookstores. On January 12, 1963, before television interviews with Rachel Carson had persuaded the American public to support her position, Merton wrote to Carson, congratulating her on her "fine, exact and persuasive book" (WF 70).[12] Merton had for some time been concerned about racism, war, nuclear weapons, and the dangers of technology.[13] He had been in contact with the reconciliation proponent James Forest, peace activist Daniel Berrigan, and two nonviolence advocates, Jean Goss and Hildegard Goss-Mayr. Peace and the moral bankruptcy of the Vietnam War were uppermost in his mind. And yet Merton paused to initiate a contact with Rachel Carson. Why might this be? What revelation of justice was tugging at Merton's heart?

A careful reading of Merton's letter to Carson reveals several points of resonance with her, namely, her prophetic stance, her ability to view the significance of research on the macro scale of human decision making, and her belief in the interdependence of all creation. When Merton writes that *Silent Spring* is "perhaps much more timely even than you or I realize," he is sensing in Carson a kindred spirit who is offering both information and insight on the cutting edge of an issue: information with far-reaching consequences, and profound insight into our responsibility for the Earth. "Though you are treating of just one aspect, and a rather detailed aspect, of our technological civilization," writes Merton, "you are, perhaps without altogether realizing, contributing a most valuable and essential piece of evidence for the diagnosis of the ills of our civilization." How keen an observation! The misuse of DDT represents more than the negative effects of one chemical; it symbolizes something askew in our twisted view of creation. Merton realized that Carson's research offered the perfect illustration of how we not only disregard the value of small things such as garden pests, but also exhibit "portentous irresponsibility" on the grand scale, that is, in world politics and war. He comments:

> We dare to use our titanic power in a way that threatens not only civilization but life itself. The same mental processing, I almost said mental illness, seems to be at work in both cases, and your book makes it clear to me that there is a *consistent pattern* running through everything that we do, through every aspect of our culture, our thought, our economy, our whole way of life. What this pattern is I cannot say clearly, but I believe it is now the most vitally important thing for all of us . . . to try to arrive at a clear, cogent statement of our ills, so that we may begin to correct them. . . . It seems that our remedies are instinctively those which aggravate the sickness: *the*

jhs

ABBEY OF GETHSEMANI
TRAPPIST, KENTUCKY

Jan 12, 1963

Dear Rachel Carson:

[Houghton Mifflin's publicity manager, and friend of Merton]
Ann Ford very kindly sent me your latest book, SILENT SPRING, which I am
reading carefully and with great concern. I want to tell you first of all that
I compliment you on the fine, exact and persuasive book you have written, and
secondly that it is perhaps much more timely even than you or I realize. Though
you are treating of just one aspect, and a rather detailed aspect, of our technological civilization, you are, perhaps without altogether realizing, contributing a
most valuable and essential piece of evidence for the diagnosis of the ills of our
civilization.

The awful irresponsibility with which we scorn the smallest values is part of
the same portentous irresponsibility with which we dare to use our titanic power
in a way that threatens  not only civilization but life itself. The same mental
processes, I almost said mental illness, seems to be at work in both cases, and
your book makes it clear to me that there is a consistent pattern running through
everything that we do, through every aspect of our culture, our thought, our
economy, our whole way of life. What this pattern is I cannot say clearly, but
I believe it is now the most vitally important thing for all of us, however
we may be concerned with our society, to try to arrive at a clear, cogent statement
of our ills, so that we may begin to correct them. Otherwise, our efforts will be
directed at purely superficial symptoms only, and perhaps not even at things related
directly to the illness. On the contrary, it seems that our remedies are instinctively
those which aggravate the sickness: the remedies are expressions of the sickness
itself.

I would almost dare to say that the sickness is perhaps a very real and very
dreadful hatred of life as such, of course subconscious, buried under our pitiful
and superficial optimism about ourselves and our affluent society. But I think that
the very thought processes of materialistic affluence ( and here the same things are
found in all the different economic systems that seek affluence for its own sake)
are ultimately self defeating. They contain so many built in frustrations that they
inevitably lead us to despair in the midst of "plenty" and "happiness" and the awful
fruit of this despair is indiscriminate, irresponsible destructiveness, hatred of
life, carried on in the name of life itself. In order to "survive" we instinctively
destroy that on which our survival depends.

Another thought that has struck me with powerful impact on reading your book:
together with my friends Erich Fromm and D.T.Suzuki, I have been absorbed in the
idea of the mythical and poetic expression of the doctrine of the "fall" of man
and original sin. The pattern in the Genesis account is very instructive. It seems to
indicate that the meaning of original sin, whatever may be ones dogmatic
convictions about it, is that man has built in to himself a tendency to destroy
and negate himself when everything is at its best, and that it is just when things
are paradisiacal that he uses this power. The whole world itself, to religious
thinkers, has always appeared as a transparent manifestation of the love of God,
as a "paradise" of His wisdom, manifested in all His creatures, down to the tiniest,
and in the wonderful interrelationship between them.

Letter to Rachel Carson from Thomas Merton

Man's vocation was to be in this cosmic creation so to speak as the eye in the body. What I say now is a religious, not a scientific statement. That is to say man is at once a part of nature, and he transcends it. In maintaining this delicate balance, he must make use of nature wisely, and understand his position, ultimately relating both himself and visible nature to the invisible -in my terms, to the Creator, in any case, to the source and exemplar of all being and all life.

But man has lost his "sight" and is blundering around aimlessly in the midst of the wonderful works of God. It is in thinking that he sees, in gaining power and technical know how, that he has lost his wisdom and his cosmic perspective. I see this clearly too in books like those of Laurens Van Der Post about the South African Bushmen. I am sure you must have read some of them.

Technics and wisdom are not by any means opposed. On the contrary, the duty of our age, the critical "vocation" of modern man is to unite them in a supreme humility which will result in a totally self forgetful creativity and service. Can we do this? Certainly we are not going in the right direction. But a book like yours is a most salutary and important warning. I desperately hope that everyone who has a chance to help form public opinion on these vital practical matters may read your book. I hope also that lawmakers will be able to see the connection between what you say and the vastly more important problem of nuclear war: the relationship is so terribly close. It is exactly the same kind of "logic". We don't like the looks of a Japanese beetle. We let ourselves be convinced by a salesman that the beetle is a dire threat. It then becomes obvious that the thing to do is exterminate the beetle by any means whatever even if it means the extermination of many other beings which have not harmed us and which even bring joy into our lives: worse still, we will exterminate the beetle even if it means danger to our children and to our very selves. To make this seem "reasonable" we go to some lengths lengths to produce arguments that our steps are really "harmless"

I am afraid I do not relish the safety of the atomic age, but I hope I can use it to attain to a salutary detachment from life and from temporal things so that I can dedicate myself entirely and freely to truth and to my fellow man. A dangerous situation after all has certain spiritual advantages. Let us hope that we may be guided effectively in the right directions.

I want to conclude by sending you my very best wishes and every expression of personal esteem. I love your books, and I love the nature that is all around me here. And I regret my own follies with DDT, which I have now totally renounced.

All blessings to you for the new year.

*Thomas Merton*

PS Sometime I would like to write to you about some of our problems here. Cedar trees dying out unaccountably, an awful plague of bagworms, etc etc.

*If you like I can send you an ms book of mine on nuclear war - mimeographed.*

*remedies are expressions of the sickness itself.* I would almost dare to say that the sickness is perhaps a very real and very dreadful hatred of life. (WF 70–71)

The canker in our society is "hatred of life"? What an indictment. Merton himself was astute at reading the signs of the times and delineating the long-range implications of human activity. In the later part of the 1950s and into the 1960s Merton had been reflecting and writing on the rights of indigenous people, the dangers of technology, atomic energy and nuclear war, the Christian responsibility for peacemaking, and the urgent need for the practice of nonviolence as a means toward peace.[14] Fifteen months earlier, Merton, the first Roman Catholic cleric to speak publicly against the Vietnam War, had made a definitive entry into this struggle with an essay on the madness of war published in the *Catholic Worker*: "The Root of War Is Fear." Most of this essay appears also as a chapter in the theologically updated and revised *New Seeds of Contemplation*.[15] With rhetorical conviction Merton castigates us for our "fictional thinking" bent on creating "a scapegoat in whom we have invested all the evil in the world"; he challenges Western civilization to relinquish its false notion of superiority and accompanying hatred of the "Other" (NSC 114).

In Merton's mind our propensity for nuclear war and our desire to eradicate garden pests spring from the same hubris. To make his point to Carson that we have relinquished wisdom in favor of technology, Merton creates an analogy between our radical actions to exterminate the Japanese beetle, that "dire threat," and our ability and determination to exterminate the enemy through nuclear war. Both, insists Merton, rely on the same logic. Once we have labeled a nonhuman species or human being as Other, we arrogantly believe in our right to eradicate the undesirable. "In order to 'survive' we instinctively destroy that on which our survival depends." Regardless of the collateral damage, we believe chemicals for pest control and weaponry to eliminate human pests are justified—even desirable. Despite the danger to nature, to ourselves, and to our children, government leaders and politicians are bent on convincing us that our actions are "harmless." Merton traces our "awful irresponsibility" and instinctive propensity for destructiveness to "the doctrine of the 'fall' of man and original sin"—a pattern that, "whatever may be one's dogmatic convictions about it, . . . man has built in to himself a tendency to destroy and negate himself when everything is at its best, and that it is just when things are paradisiacal that he uses this power." Such obstinacy and perverse blindness has been dubbed by the writer Barbara Kingsolver contemporary society's "crisis of perception."[16] Yet there is hope. Merton acknowledges his interdependent vision—what Christian theologians might label an incarnational vision—that is, a recognition of a Spirit-filled world from the first moments of Creation, the invitation to acknowledge our common relatedness in Jesus, and our unique human vocation that carries with it privileges and responsibilities.[17] "The whole world itself, to religious thinkers," writes Merton, "has always appeared as a transparent manifestation of the love of God, as a 'paradise' of His wisdom, manifested in all His creatures, down to the tiniest, and in the most wonderful interrelationship between them. . . . That is to say, man is at once a part of nature and he transcends it. In maintaining this delicate balance, he must make use of nature wisely." Elaborating on his point, Merton maintains that our vocation is "to be in this cosmic creation, so to speak, as the eye in the body," a vocation to defend and preserve the "delicate balance" in nature. Unfortunately, "man has lost his 'sight' and is blundering around aimlessly in the midst of the wonderful works of God" (WF 71).

Such a statement in the 1960s emphasizes Merton's own prophetic awareness of his unique human dignity and interdependence with all creatures on this planet. In his view all creation is part of the unfolding love of God, and each being reveals a unique aspect of the Divine. Grounding his thinking, as he admits to Carson, in his reading of the psychologist Erich Fromm and Zen scholar D. T. Suzuki, Merton distances himself from a Cartesian mechanistic and compartmentalized view of the world. He reiterates the importance of maintaining a "cosmic perspective"—a broad vision that sees all creation as relationship, and human dignity springing from a true sense of our shared creature-hood. Merton would have us reject hubris in favor of humility, a word whose root is *humus,* earthiness—a recognition of both the clay and stardust that we are. His position echoes Carson's: "Wonder and humility are wholesome emotions, and they do not exist side by side with a lust for destruction."[18] This paradox of plainness and exalted dignity appears elsewhere in Merton's prose and poetry. For example, in his poem "O Sweet Irrational Worship," he proclaims:

> I have become light,
> Bird and wind!
> My leaves sing.
> I am earth, earth.

And in "Love Winter When the Plant Says Nothing," Merton reminds us how "Secret/Vegetal words" and "Unlettered water" are to be reverenced for their silent, unnoticed growth occurring even in the paradox of apparently dead winter (CP 344, 353).

In each instance Merton is recognizing and celebrating a vision of creation not shared by many of his contemporaries. His letter to Rachel Carson is more than a congratulatory message to a well-known writer; it is a revelation of his long-held incarnational vision that acknowledges the divine spark in all creation, making each creature holy and worthy of respect. Such an expanding vision is critical to deep spiritual growth. If one pitches a tent in the wilderness, for example, one gains a certain perspective on the world through the tent flaps; if those tent pegs are shifted, that vision can be enlarged. Merton's letter to Carson marks such a significant enlargement of vision. Having focused his social justice writing on right relationships among people—topics of racism, the rights of indigenous people, the dangers of atomic energy and technology, as well as the moral imperative for making peace through nonviolent means—Merton is now articulating a new insight: responsibility for the Earth.

It is significant that in the final paragraph of his letter to Carson, Merton regrets his "own follies with DDT, which I have now totally renounced" and includes a postscript indicating a desire to consult

Carson later on the monastery's problems with bagworms in their cedar trees. From almost any perspective, reading *Silent Spring* is a graced
moment in Merton's life—because Carson's book appears to have allowed him to see how human justice is related to ecojustice. I use the
word "appears" deliberately because this letter to Carson is Merton's
first public utterance—as much as a personal letter is public—about
nonviolence to the environment. It might seem that Carson is solely
responsible for shocking or widening Merton's vision of social justice
to include all species of creation, nonhuman as well as human. It could
be argued, however, that Merton's life experiences—his early childhood in France, the events recorded in *The Seven Storey Mountain,* the
insights expressed and explored in his many poems and journals, his
longtime fascination with Gandhi, as well as his own commitment to
contemplation—predisposed him to this particular moment of seeing
differently, an increased awareness that the Buddhist practitioner Thích
Nhat Hanh calls "engaged spirituality."[19] Even so, Merton's letter to
Carson represents a defining moment that signals a personal revolution
already under way, namely, a deepening sense of environmental justice.

In 1963, when he wrote to Rachel Carson, Merton had been a
Trappist monk for more than twenty years. His academic training in
literature, his natural gift for writing, and his extended experience in
theology and contemplation made him a responsive reader of *Silent
Spring.* Although from different backgrounds and fields, Carson and
Merton had discovered important characteristics of life on this planet.
Carson's professional life, which involved intense training in observation of sea life as well research and extensive publications for the Bureau
of Fisheries, led to her vision of the interdependence of all creation and
the human challenge of acting for wholeness; Merton's monastic life,
which also involved intense training in awareness, led to an expanded
vision of our complete dependence on God, our interdependence with
each other, and the challenge of acting in nonviolent ways toward all
creation. Carson's discipline was marine biology; Merton's was silence
and solitude. Carson's practice of the scientific method prepared her to
confront the problem of dying songbirds; Merton's practice of regular
communal prayer and extended periods of individual contemplation

prepared him to embrace the world and its problems with compassion and justice. Carson's love for the world, coupled with a love of words and a flourishing literary career, enabled her to write graceful, persuasive, astute books that contributed to the field of nature writing, made her the most noted science writer in America, and, in the case of *Silent Spring*, triggered modern environmental thinking;[20] Merton's love for the world, coupled with a fascination and facility for words and commitment to the Word (*Logos*), enabled him to inspire thousands with his writing on spirituality, prayer, and East-West dialogue, and stretched him in his later years to see how justice for human beings must of necessity include justice for the planet.

In both writers there is a sense of responsibility for environmental health that comes from attentiveness to their surroundings and commitment to a coherent vision of the cosmos. In both writers there is what the ecocritic Jonathan Bate has called *ecopoesis*—a deep longing for belonging.[21] In such sensitive writers, argues Bate, the rhythm of words—their syntactic connections and linguistic overtones—are intimately related to the "song of the earth itself."[22] Indeed, external and internal landscapes merge when the healing and integration that words can evoke challenge us to apply these same principles of wholeness to the place in which we dwell. Both Carson and Merton were pondering the essential question, traceable to American nature writers as early as the 1790s and persisting today: How shall we live? How shall we or can we belong?[23] In light of new scientific data, both writers—Merton and Carson—saw the urgency of attempting an answer to that question. For Carson the answer could be found in human action: diminishing the use of chemical pesticides in favor of biological controls; for Merton the answer was beginning to dawn on him that nonviolence to the Earth means we must develop an ecological conscience.

It might seem curious that this impassioned response was to a book whose effect was barely beginning to grow from a gentle ripple to the veritable tidal wave of public sentiment it would become—and yet, not so curious. Rachel Carson had written a landmark book that would influence millions and trigger the first American legislation intended to preserve the health of our environment. Her revelation about the negative effects of DDT not only on plants and animals, but on the human body, initiated a revolution in American thinking that underlies our current notion of ecojustice. Early on that journey, she touched the consciousness and heart of Thomas Merton, a writer and monk, with a revelation of justice for the planet that engendered its own on-going revolution of love in his thinking and writing—a revolution of love that expanded to include not just human beings but the entire planetary community.

What might have prepared Merton for this singular moment of grace? What in his life had developed in him a habit of seeing and an awareness that enabled and supported this major shift in understanding when he read Carson's book? How could a master of contemplation allow a petite marine biologist and popular nature writer to be a provocateur who would set him on a discernible path toward stronger environmental responsibility? Obviously, seeds planted by God in Merton's experience were coming to fruition during that turn of the year from 1962 to 1963. As Merton himself had written, "Every moment and every event of every man's life on earth plants something in his soul" (NSC 14). Chapter 2 probes Merton's early life, looking for examples of those seeds: influences and patterns that contributed to his predisposition for ecological thinking. Central to these influences was a readiness to allow geography—what modern nature writers call "a sense of place"—to shape his thinking and spiritual development.

*Chapter 2*

# Learning to See
## Becoming Awake

New eyes awaken . . .
And I am drunk with the great wilderness
Of the sixth day in Genesis.
—Thomas Merton, "A Psalm"

It's all about seeing—not merely looking, but *seeing*. Seeing with new eyes. Awakening to one's surroundings and cultivating awareness of both external and internal movements of grace. Yet the development from looking to seeing does not happen automatically; it requires conscious effort and focus—sometimes even training—and often results in a transformation of consciousness. Writers, prophets, and poets through the centuries have challenged us to develop the habit of seeing and the art of attention so that transformation might occur. Indeed, all major religions exhort their followers to engage in a process of becoming awake.

Buddhism, for example, traces its origin to Siddhartha Gautama, the one who woke up and urged his followers to do the same; Hinduism, with its reliance on the Vedic path to holiness (and specifically Upanishadic thought), encourages each person to reawaken the connection with God in order to discover Absolute Truth. Islam, from the Arabic word meaning "submission," calls believers to continual awareness of God through prayer five times a day. Judaism professes faith in the coming of Shalom, or Peace, which will inaugurate a total transformation of human life and the natural world into justice and peace—a work of God and humans as cocreators to which one must

22

always be attentive. Christianity, Merton's own adopted tradition, invites practitioners to awareness of God's unconditional love by imitating Jesus, who models how to realize this divine potential. In Roman Catholic liturgy, for example, important feast days are preceded by a Vigil, which may involve a fast or special readings to encourage followers to be "vigilant," watchful, awake; and the entire season of Advent invites Christians to become more attentive, more alert—to enter into the great Christian paradox: waiting for the One who is already here yet who is always coming to us. In centuries past, Bach and Handel captured this spirit of focused anticipation with the haunting cantata *Wachet auf* (Sleepers, Wake) and the soul-stirring oratorio *Messiah*.

Becoming awake—seeing with new eyes—is never a passive event. A human being is not a tabula rasa to be imprinted with sight and insight from some external and detached source. Becoming awake is meant to be a participatory endeavor that involves a response, namely, recognition of the deeper meaning of an event. To draw an example, again from Christian tradition: Christmas is not meant to be a stand-alone celebration of gaping fondly at a baby in a manger, but a prelude to the mystery's fulfillment, poignantly symbolized by Mary Magdalene's recognition of the resurrected Jesus in the garden and her mission to spread the Good News. Although we frequently hear the beautiful strains of Handel's *Messiah* during the Advent season and mistakenly associate it with Christmas, this great oratorio's Easter section completes the retelling of the Christian mystery. It must be noted that the mighty and well-loved "Hallelujah Chorus" occurs not in the Christmas section, but near the celebratory end of the oratorio as a response to the great feast and feat of the Redemption of humankind.[1]

## Becoming Awake

So too, in normal human development, seeing with new eyes—becoming awake—requires us to respond with the vigor of recognition. Seeing anew, experiencing a new consciousness, is the prelude to expanded vision. This is not a completely novel notion. Literary artists and mystics in different ages have offered testimony to the power of "attentive" seeing—that is, a kind of seeing that is more than mere looking. The British engraver and poet William Blake insisted that his childhood experience of seeing a tree full of angels guided him in his artistic expression and revisionist Christian theology. At the height of the American Transcendentalist movement in the 1830s and 1840s, Ralph Waldo Emerson and Henry David Thoreau urged us to see the natural world with new eyes and commit to a worldview radically different from the prevailing Calvinist attitude that regarded the wilderness as evil. Emerson's famous lines about being alert to the spiritual world surrounding each of us immediately come to mind: "Standing on the bare ground—my head bathed by the blithe air and uplifted into infinite space,—all mean egotism vanishes. I become a transparent eyeball; I am nothing; I see all; the currents of the Universal Being circulate through me; I am part or particle of God. . . . I am a lover of uncontained and immortal beauty. In the wilderness, I find something more dear and connate than in streets or villages. In the tranquil landscape, and especially in the distant line of the horizon, man beholds somewhat as beautiful as his own nature."[2]

"I become a transparent eyeball." Certainly not a graceful metaphor, but one that makes its point. Becoming a "seer" means emptying oneself in order to recognize and receive the spiritual message inherent in created reality—something akin to the poet John Keats's concept of "negative capability," that is, an ability to empty oneself of all predispositions and preconceptions, and with intentional open-mindedness absorb totally the ambiguities and uncertainties of the moment.[3] Likewise, in *Walden,* Thoreau's 1854 published meditation on his retreat of two years, two months, and two days in the wilderness, the author is explicit about his purpose: to call his Concord neighbors to wake up. He proclaims himself a chanticleer urging greater alertness to the ever-new natural world surrounding us and concludes his carefully constructed and highly revised text with a call to action: "Only that day dawns to which we are awake. There is more day to dawn. The sun is but a morning star."[4] The naturalist John Burroughs in his seminal 1908 essay, "The Art of Seeing Things," makes the point that while some people appear to have "buttons or painted marbles" for eyes, others—with either "practice or inspiration"—become metaphorical sharpshooters with a keen eye that "selects and discriminates." For such fortunate humans, the "power of attention is always on the alert, not by conscious effort, but by natural habit and disposition."[5]

Yet American writers are not the only possessors of the secret of becoming awake and of seeing differently. In the third century, long before any literary or social movement had arisen, the Desert Mothers and Fathers recommended the practice of *agrupnia,* a spiritual discipline of wakefulness and self-emptying that often produced an experience of mysticism. As the theologian Belden Lane has noted, "The desert, as a place where one expects nothing, becomes the source of the hauntingly unexpected."[6] Medieval Christian mystics, as well, celebrated the power of seeing and recognizing the holy in all creation and the fundamental unity of all beings. Julian of Norwich reveals God's intimate message as a call to intentional alertness; Hildegard of Bingen and Mechtilde of Magdeburg remind us that we know God through every created creature; and the scholastic theologian Thomas Aquinas declares, "Every creature participates in some way in the likeness of the Divine Essence."[7] In more recent times, the twentieth-century mystic Simone Weil maintained that every true artist's intimate contact with the world of sights and sounds is like a sacrament. Traditionally, *sacrament* has been defined as a visible sign that reveals and communicates grace.[8] Yet, insists Weil, whether or not one finds God, the act of looking and waiting with open eyes is essential to realizing our full human potential. "Looking," she says, "is what saves us."[9]

Thomas Merton was not unacquainted with this transformative journey of learning to see with new eyes. In addition to what might be considered the normal trajectory of developing human consciousness, Merton possessed the ability to use moments of seeing as grist for expanding his consciousness. From his childhood days of trudging after his father, Owen, on painting forays, to his fascination with Byzantine mosaics in the churches of Rome, to his master's thesis on the concept of beauty in the works of William Blake, to his final days in Polonnaruwa when, in the presence of the great Buddhas, he realized he was now "beyond the shadow and the disguise" (OSM 323), Merton intentionally exercised his gift of awareness—a practice the artist and spiritual director Marianne Hieb calls "receptive seeing" and "contemplative gazing,"[10] and one the writer Mark Nepo defines as the freshness and power of "first sight."[11] Each event and place expanded Merton's belief in the value of *seeing* the uniqueness of each creature and acknowledging the sacredness of place. Merton understood in the depths of his being the importance of William Blake's aphorism about the need to see clearly: "If the doors of perception were cleansed, we would see man as he is, infinite."[12] A reader of Blake, Merton frequently alluded to this British Romantic poet's wisdom. Blake's oft-quoted dictum, for example—"Everything that is, is holy"—is a chapter title in *Seeds of Contemplation* (1949) and its revision as *New Seeds of Contemplation* (1962). Events, experiences, and places deepened a habit of awareness in Merton, enabling him in 1955 to assert in *No Man Is an Island*: "The first step in the interior life, nowadays, is not, as some might imagine, learning not to see and taste and hear and feel things. On the contrary, what we must do is begin by unlearning our wrong ways of seeing, tasting, feeling, and so forth, and acquire a few of the right ones."[13] In Merton's journal for May 31, 1961, we find an ongoing affirmation of the necessity of this dynamic process: "Again, sense of the importance, the urgency of seeing, fully aware, experiencing what is *here*: not what is given by men, by society, but what is given by God and hidden by (even monastic) society. Clear realization that I must begin with these first elements. That it is absurd to inquire after my function in the world, or whether I have one, as long as I am not first of all alive and awake" (TTW 123).

One is tempted to coin a new Eastern koan that Merton would enjoy ruminating over: If one is awake, can one become more awake? This paradox suggests that one *can* become more alert, more attentive, more awake to the external world as well as to the action of God holding us in being and nudging us toward fuller humanness. In "The Art of Seeing Things," John Burroughs asserts, "Power of attention and a mind sensitive to outward objects, in these lies the secret of seeing things."[14] Mark Nepo declares: "First sight is the moment of God-sight, heart-sight, soul-sight. It is the seeing of revelation, the feeling of oneness that briefly overcomes us when nothing remains in the way."[15] And Marianne Hieb reminds us that this kind of "receptive seeing will always hold out the possibility of surprise." At its core, she writes, "noticing is a state of mind, a willingness to keep the questions open. Your noticing deepens the contemplative presence essential to all creative processes."[16] Discovering this secret of seeing and becoming more awake is what impels Merton to share his experience in poems such as "In Silence," in which he counsels:

> Be still.
> Listen to the stones of the wall.
> Be silent, they try
> To speak your
> Name.

And in that stillness, that deeper awareness, discover "All their si-lence / Is on fire" (CP 280–81). Discovering this secret is also what underpins Merton's 1963 lament to Rachel Carson that human beings have lost their sight and are "blundering around aimlessly in the midst of the wonderful works of God" (WF 71).

In a recent book on Merton as a "master of attention," Robert Waldron offers us a powerful vignette of the twenty-four-year-old Merton as art critic—one who sees outward objects and sees beyond the obvious. Citing passages from Merton's premonastic journal de-scribing the 1939 World's Fair in New York City and in particular his response to Fra Angelico's *Temptation of St. Anthony* and Bruegel's *The Wedding Dance*, Waldron deems Merton's perceptive critique of these masterpieces to be an act of pure attention. Merton, he argues, has discovered how to look; at the end of the passage on Fra Angelico Merton confesses: "Looking at this picture is exactly the same sort of thing as praying" (RM 53). Without directly quoting Duns Sco-tus's philosophy on *haecceitas,* that is, the "thisness" of things, Mer-ton demonstrates he is capable of zeroing in on the uniqueness of the artist's vision. Waldron suggests that since Merton had no great art to look at after entering the monastery, he needs to find beauty

*Where do I find beauty here, in this place?*

in the fluidity of Gregorian chant, the timeless ritual of the Catholic Latin Mass, the meditative slowness of *lectio divina*, and the natural beauty of the Kentucky hills.[17] And, indeed those Kentucky hills were a distinctive gift that enhanced Merton's spirituality. But this gift had several antecedents in Merton's early life—specific geographies—that prepared him for the influence of nature on his monastic spirituality and experience of contemplation.

## Growing Awareness of Place

Just as a habit of *seeing* and specific events can significantly influence our level of awareness, so too can geography or natural landscape (e.g., mountains, desert, seashore) have a lasting effect on our developing consciousness. The nature writer Barry Lopez offers persuasive testimony to this phenomenon, which, when applied to Thomas Merton, reveals new avenues of understanding about the transformative journey of becoming awake. On the basis of his extensive interaction with indigenous people, Lopez contends that geography or place is not a "subject" but a shaping force on imagination—our powers of awareness—especially encounters with geography at an early age.[18] In a brief but noteworthy essay on the influence of place, Lopez explains how landscape, light, and even sound sculpt and mold our early consciousness, significantly contributing not only to our awareness, but also to our "sense of morality and human identity." As Marianne Hieb observes about external landscape, "The stuff of your life becomes the portal into the adventure of inner journeying."[19] Judging from the details of his childhood years in *The Seven Storey Mountain,* and the frequency and affection with which Merton later mentions his years in France, it is clear that the elements of this geography fashioned in him a deep sense of intimacy with place that influenced his inner journeying and later development as a monk and as a writer. Three French landscapes in particular—Prades, Saint-Antonin, Murat—as well as the city of Rome illustrate how vulnerable Merton was to the influence of geography and how deeply these places contributed in later years to his love of wilderness and his evolving ecological consciousness.

## Prades

"On the last day of January 1915, under the sign of the Water Bearer, in a year of a great war, and down in the shadow of some French mountains on the borders of Spain, I came into the world"—the opening lines of Merton's autobiography, *The Seven Storey Mountain* (SSM 3). Anyone who visits Prades, France, where Merton was born, will be forcefully struck by the quaintness of this village, dominated by its sacred, snow-capped Canigou Mountain, the monasteries tucked into the terraced hillsides, and the all-pervasive startling light that makes sunglasses and hat a necessity. Brilliant sunlight seeps down narrow, rambling streets and encircles the surrounding hills. The south of France, destination of painters for at least two centuries, is a chiaroscuro world of glaring light and looming shadow, glorious mountain air and finely honed colors. It is easy to imagine how baby Tom, just becoming aware of his world, might focus on light and color.

In *Tom's Book*, the record his mother, Ruth Jenkins Merton, was keeping for the New Zealand grandparents, she records how much little Tom was enchanted by movement and color around him.[20] In those early months, baby Tom "had already begun to wave his arms toward the landscape, crying 'Oh color!' ('Color' is the word he uses to mean landscape, his father's pictures and all the paraphernalia of painting.)" Ruth Merton also provides us with a sample *horarium* of young Tom's day, which included extensive time outdoors after his 7:30 A.M. breakfast until his bath at 10:30 A.M., and again after his 2:00 P.M. dinner until sunset. It is not unreasonable to believe that at least some of this outdoor time was spent near his father's painting sites and that patterns of light and color—from nature and from the canvas—became part of Merton's informal schooling. "When we go out," writes his mother, "he seems conscious of everything. Sometimes he puts up his arms and cries out 'Oh Sun! Oh joli!' Often it is to the birds or trees that he makes these pagan hymns of joy. Sometimes he throws himself on the ground to see the 'cunnin' little ants' (where he learned that expression, I do not know!)" (TB n.p.).

Light and color, however, are not the only shaping influence on

Young Tom. (Photo by Ruth Jenkins Merton)

imagination. Barry Lopez reminds us that the "architecture" of our world is not only visual but olfactory, tactile, auditory, and linguistic as well; these sensible experiences form a "coherence" that creates a sense of belonging.[21] Indeed, such budding coherence emerges in Ruth Merton's record of little Tom's interaction with his environment. As early as two and three months old, Ruth notices Tom saying " 'aye' in many different and expressive ways," even talking to a flower and trying to hit "a rattle swung on a string before his eyes." And by the time he is eight months old, his mother records that whenever they went "on the bridge," Tom "stood up in his p'ram, especially to see the river" (TB

Young Tom making a paper airplane, 1918. (Photo by Ruth Jenkins Merton)

n.p.). Having walked across this same bridge over the Têt River, I can readily understand why an infant—especially a precocious child like Tom, growing ever more alert to sounds, smells, and textures—would be fascinated by the river. On my stroll, I heard the river before I saw it. Like all mountain streams in close proximity to their source, the Têt catapults itself from the Pyrenees Mountains, rushing over stones, creating a symphony of white-water music.

For little Tom, the rushing river must have been like mythic sirens calling to him with secret messages, imprinting a love for water in its many forms. Perhaps the sound of the swiftly moving water was preparing him for the festival of rain he loved to hear outside the hermitage, and his recognition that people walking on shiny streets are really "walking on stars and water." Much later, in the hermitage years, Merton would write in his essay "Rain and the Rhinoceros": "What a thing it is to sit absolutely alone, in the forest, at night, cherished by this wonderful, unintelligible, perfectly innocent speech, the most comforting speech in the world, the talk that rain makes by itself all over the ridges, and the talk of the watercourses everywhere in the hollows! Nobody started it, nobody is going to stop it. It will talk as long as it wants, this rain. As long as it talks I am going to listen" (RU 10–12).

When he was just a year old, writes his mother, Tom "takes great delight in his books, knowing in just which one is the picture of the Frog, the owl or the dog and finding them for you with pleasure." After the family responded to the threat of World War I and moved to Ruth's parents' home in Douglaston, Long Island, Tom's mother overhears him carrying on a bilingual conversation with "Monsieur Wind" and imitating not only the voice of the wind but also the "Dah-hou!" of the church bells of Prades. In addition to his remarkable "powers of association," Tom, by the time he was two, had an astonishing vocabulary, astonishing even for a precocious little boy. His mother notes that he recognized and used, voluntarily and accurately, many of the names of birds and flowers such as kingfisher, chickadee, oriole, goldfinch, chrysanthemum, hollyhock, foxglove, pansy (TB n.p.).

It would not be rash to suggest that Thomas Merton was genetically predisposed to new ways of seeing because of his artistic par-

Prades, France, in a painting by Owen Merton

ents, that he was born with a keen eye that "selects and discriminates"; nevertheless, the serendipitous convergence of stunning light, natural beauty, colorful art, emerging fluency in two languages, and a mother who was consciously and conscientiously shaping and nurturing her son's interaction with his environment was a singular blessing for Merton in those first years. Prades became for Merton a sacred place—a geography where seeds were sown—that created a backdrop for later experiences. A second visit to France approximately eight years later intensified Merton's love for France and his evolving awareness of his surroundings.

## Saint-Antonin

After Ruth Merton's death from stomach cancer when Tom was six, his father valiantly tried to create educational and family experiences for Tom and his younger brother, John Paul. Leaving the younger son with his in-laws, Owen Merton and ten-year-old Tom returned to the south of France, this time to the medieval city of Saint-Antonin. After the summer months of delight in his new location, young Tom was sent some twenty miles away to the Lycée Ingres in Montauban, happily returning to Saint-Antonin on weekends and holidays. Owen Merton, now enjoying some financial success from his painting, was intent on building a home in Saint-Antonin. When the house was ready, he planned to send for John Paul, hoping to create a family again. Using stone from a nearby ruined chapel, Owen concentrated on his construction project and his painting; Tom was free to roam the tiny village, getting lost in the "labyrinth of narrow streets" that all led to the church. In his autobiography Merton remarks about the power of this place, how here—though he was not a Catholic but was surrounded by the religious ambiance of the Middle Ages—he experienced the centrality of the Christian liturgy. Although he "had no understanding of the concept of Mass," the regular, periodic church bells, the geography of the streets "and of nature itself, the circling hills, the cliffs and trees, all focussed my attention upon the one, important central fact of the church and what it contained" (SSM 36–37).

How significant that in these impressionable preadolescent years, Merton was confronted by a "whole landscape, unified by the church and its heavenward spire," that seemed to proclaim a twofold purpose: to glorify God and to remind humans of their ultimate purpose. Here, Merton says, the landscape forced him to live as a "virtual contemplative" (SSM 37). If we accept Barry Lopez's argument that awareness of geography, combined with a sense of place and unity with it, offers a fundamental defense against loneliness, perhaps it is legitimate to speculate that in Saint-Antonin Merton experienced—perhaps even savored—his first taste of real belonging, a taste that later awakened in him an appetite for contemplation and the solitude of the hermitage. Certainly, Merton was looking forward eagerly to the completion of the new house and the promise of becoming a family once again; perhaps in this sacred place he was also discovering at some deep unarticulated level of consciousness an awareness of a connection between external geography and the geography of the heart—between

Saint-Antonin, France, in a painting by Owen Merton

the French landscape and his inner landscape of thought, desire, and imagination.

## Murat

Merton's happiness in Saint-Antonin contrasted with his discomfort at the lycée in Montauban where he boarded during the school years of 1926–1927 and 1927–1928. Although Merton found it difficult to socialize with boys whose language and manners were earthy, and whom he regarded as a veritable "civilization of hyenas" (SSM 51), he did manage to earn several scholastic and athletic awards at the end of each of the school years.[22] Nevertheless, the highlight of this experience was holiday time. During Christmas 1926 and summer 1927, while Owen Merton was painting in the Auvergne district and later in Paris, Tom stayed with the Privat family in Murat, a rustic village in central France, another landscape of "rich pastures" and mountains "heavy with fir trees" that nurtured Merton's imagination and his habit of awareness (SSM 55–63). Although in his autobiography Merton expresses gratitude for the moral example offered by Monsieur and Madame Privat and treasures their simple and unconditional acceptance as a special grace, Merton also experiences the freedom to run wild in the woods and the mountains. In such a happy venue, Merton's essential loneliness was somewhat assuaged and his infant pleasure with nature reawakened and nourished. Perhaps after moving to Surrey, England, the next year with his father, a budding sense of self helped Merton through his school days at Ripley Court and a not-so-pleasant fourteenth summer spent reading and wandering the English countryside while his father was ill with a brain tumor in a hospital in London. And perhaps this budding sense of self, tied to geography, came into play again for Merton five years later in Rome, when he was truly alone, his father having died two years before.

## Rome

Shortly after his eighteenth birthday, with the blessing and monetary support from his legal guardian and Owen's classmate and physician, Tom Bennett, the orphaned Merton departed from England for the Continent. Having walked through the French Riviera and suffered the humiliation of having to request more money from his guardian, Merton finally arrived in Rome, where he spent most of his time reading and visiting antiquities—as he describes it in his autobiography, free but miserable (SSM 106).

Eventually Merton found himself visiting old churches, fascinated by the frescoes and Byzantine Christian mosaics, a world of art that celebrated Jesus as *Logos,* the Word spoken by the Father. These mosaics, he admits, "told me more than I had ever known of the doctrine of a God of infinite power, wisdom, and love Who had yet become Man" (SSM 110). As in his infancy, Merton was once again captivated by color, especially the startling mosaic of Christ coming in judgment in the Church of Saints Cosmas and Damian across from the Forum. The "dark blue sky, with a suggestion of fire in the small clouds beneath His feet" must have yanked Merton's memory to other natural and painted landscapes he had loved as a child. The contrast between the "vapid, boring, semi-pornographic statuary of the Empire" he had been looking at and this "art full of spiritual vitality and earnestness and power" was a moment of transformation (SSM 108). Merton admits he became a pilgrim to these churches, not yet seeking spiritual nourishment, but abandoning his adolescent malaise for the new awareness of and inner peace produced by religious art. His ability to see, to be awake to his surroundings, drew him to this world of Byzantine Christianity and its emphasis on Christ as *Logos.* With a nascent sense of homecoming, Merton began reading the Bible and extending his list of favorite churches—not yet experiencing a conversion, but laying the groundwork for another transforming moment of grace. That grace—a spiritual experience of his father, dead for more than two years—came one evening in Merton's rented room.

In his autobiography Merton describes an awareness of his father's presence in chiaroscuro terms that are reminiscent of the sharp contrasts of light and shadow in southern France. Merton recalls that the night was dark; the light in his room was on. Suddenly, the strong presence of Owen Merton "was as vivid and as real and as startling as if he had touched my arm or spoken to me. . . . I was overwhelmed with a sudden and profound insight into the misery and corruption of my own soul, and I was pierced deeply with a light that made me realize something of the condition I was in." Through tears and prayer—for the first time ever "praying out of the very roots of my life and of my being, and praying to the God I had never known"—Merton begged God to "reach down towards me out of His darkness" to free him of his shackles of selfishness. The next morning, impelled by the intensity of this experience, his "soul broken up with contrition," Merton headed for the Dominican Church of Santa Sabina, one of his favorites, and walked "deliberately into the church with no other purpose than to kneel down and pray to God." At the altar rail, with "all the belief" he had in him, Merton slowly recited the Our Father—a prayer he had not said since his childhood in Douglaston, Long Island. Then Merton looked about the church, revisited the room with a painting by Sassoferrato, and poked his head out the door overlooking a lovely garden "where the sun shone down on an orange tree." Feeling reborn, Merton strolled to a nearby deserted church and a field where he sat "in the sun, on a wall and tasted the joy of my own inner peace" (SSM 111–13).

Why Santa Sabina for this dramatic moment of grace, one in a series of conversions that eventually led Merton to Catholicism and to the Trappist monastery? Having spent time looking at the setting and interior of this church, I want to suggest three possible reasons based on its natural geography and architecture: the intimacy of the Aventine Hill; the startling light in the nave; and the welcoming mosaics. The Church of Santa Sabina is reached by climbing a winding cobblestone street, suggestive of the seclusion offered by villages in southern France. Once inside the classical basilica with its original cypress doors, the visitor is immediately struck by the bright light from the clerestory—a startling contrast to the dark churches that dot the Roman cityscape. Both of these physical features may have been drawing cards for the orphaned and wandering Merton, evoking memories of Prades and the stirring light of southern France. In addition, the impressive fifth-century mosaics over the entrance doors are untainted by the later baroque influence on religious architecture. If, as Antoine de Saint-Exupéry reminds us, it is only with the heart that one sees rightly, these mosaics depicting the Church of the Circumcised and the Church of the Gentiles may have been subtly signaling to Merton the welcoming possibility of inclusion and belonging. The art he had been enjoying for its color and light, combined with Merton's "contemplative gazing" and receptivity to this hauntingly familiar landscape, may have burst into new spiritual awareness—recognition of where his heart really needed to reside.

Barry Lopez's preconditions for landscape to influence one's imagination and create a deep sense of place are present in this startling episode: silence, intense feeling, and a recognition of the complex significance of an experience that goes beyond simple analysis.[23] Surely Merton's extended time by himself, as a child and now as a young man, orphaned and searching for focus, provided him with ample time for silence, awareness of his inner loneliness, and an affinity for the comfort of place. In Saint-Antonin Merton had begun to discover an inner spirituality, rudimentary, to be sure, but in Murat he learned to be a companion of place, achieving some inner relationship with and feeling for the hills. In Rome he experienced what Wordsworth called a "gentle shock of mild surprise," an emotional intensity that both terrified and freed him because of its unexplainable and penetrating significance.[24] In short, attentiveness to his surroundings—that is, being *present* and vulnerable to the details of landscape, the power of place—not only bolsters a habit of awareness, but also begins to create coherence between inner and outer geographies, between the external landscape and the landscape of the heart.

## Prelude to the Monastery

This sequence of significant experiences of color, light, sound, and particular geographies became a handful of spiritual seeds germinating during Merton's years at Columbia University. In New York City he was again immersed in color, shapes, and words. Frenetic activity and the late-night buzz of innovative ideas stimulated his thinking. In addition to classes and time spent drinking, listening to jazz, hanging out with friends—Bob Lax, Ed Rice, Ad Reinhardt, and Seymour Freedgood—Merton spent hours as a member of the literary and debating society, editor of the yearbook, and art editor for the *Jester*, the campus humor magazine. His cartoons of this period suggest a fertile mind, alive to shapes, contours, and quirks of the human animal.

Merton was also reading broadly and deeply. In addition to pivotal books by Etienne Gilson (*The Spirit of Medieval Philosophy*) and Aldous Huxley (*Ends and Means*), which opened his mind to the logic and mysticism of Catholicism, Merton met Mahanambrata Brahmachari in January 1938, a Hindu monk who encouraged him to investigate his own spiritual roots. Expanding his reading to include classic texts of Catholicism such as *The Confessions of St. Augustine* and *The Imitation of Christ,* Merton was also attracted to the life and work of William Blake, eventually writing his master's thesis on Blake's avant-garde theory of art. Surely several of Blake's paradoxical proverbs from "The Marriage of Heaven and Hell" could have been guiding principles for Merton's college life: "Without Contraries, there is no Progression" and "The road of excess leads to the palace of wisdom."[25] Merton's deeply embedded interest in words is evident, too, in his fondness for the poetry of Gerard Manley Hopkins and his intent to write a doctoral dissertation on Hopkins's poetry. His fascination with words extended into his summers, often spent at Bob Lax's family cottage in Olean, New York, where Merton and his friends were each trying to write the great American novel. The hills of southwestern New York that Merton came to love for their beauty and peace, and their contrast to the urban concrete of New York City, must have reminded him of those halcyon days in France when he was free to read, write stories, and roam the countryside.

At this same time Merton was attracted to the Franciscan spirit of unity with nature and its respect for Brother Sun and Sister Moon. Shortly after his conversion to Roman Catholicism and baptism in Corpus Christi Church in November 1938, Merton felt drawn to the priesthood and considered joining the Franciscans. But when this path became a dead end, he accepted a teaching position at St. Bonaventure College (now University)—not out of reach for a visit to the World's Fair in New York City and the intensity of *seeing* he called a kind of praying. At St. Bonaventure, Merton could immerse himself in the natural beauty of the Alleghany hills, words, jazz, and his newfound love for the Breviary (or Divine Office, now referred to as Liturgy of the Hours), reciting psalms at appointed hours of the day in unison with the praying monastic church. Often, in the "deep untrodden drifts [of snow] along the wood's edge, toward the river," Merton recited the Hours under a canopy of trees that formed a "noiseless, rudimentary church," causing him to reflect about this sacred space: "What miles of silences God has made in you for contemplation! If only people realized what all your mountains and forests are really for!" (SSM 309–10).

But Merton was edgy, looking for something to fill the hole in his orphan's heart. At the suggestion of Dan Walsh, his former teacher-mentor at Columbia, Merton made a Holy Week retreat in 1941 at the Abbey of Gethsemani, in Kentucky. Merton was captivated— captivated by the beauty of the liturgy and by the rigor of the Trappist lifestyle. He believed that loving God meant giving all to God. Back at St. Bonaventure, struggling with what direction his life would take, he heard in his imagination the monastery tower bell signaling the end of night prayer. "The bell seemed to be telling me where I belonged—as if it were calling me home" (SSM 365). But herein lay a conundrum: Could Merton relinquish his love of nature—what he thought of as his Franciscan spirit—to become a Trappist? Merton's journal entry for September 4, 1941, reveals his disquiet and eventual resolve:

> One thing seems to be clear: that, when I was at Gethsemani, I nearly ruined my retreat with wondering whether or not it was possible I could even have a vocation to be a Trappist—and, if so, if I would be able to stand the discipline all my life. . . . The only answer to that is: there is nothing in the Trappist discipline to prevent you loving nature the way I meant it then and do now: loving it in God's creation, and a sign of His goodness and Love. . . . All things that are, are good, just because they have being. Their being is a gift, and it is therefore a sign of love: God so loves all things that He creates them, and so loves us He gives us being, and so loves us that though in our murderous ingratitude we murder our loving being with our pride, then He recreates us, making His own Son flesh to dwell among us. (RM 399–400)

Merton here is making a distinction between creation—the "production" of God—and nature: all life forms in general. In subsequent years he would come to realize that an artificial dualism of subject/object is inadequate for his prayer and embrace. Yet at this moment in a gesture of giving all to God, even before he officially entered the monastery, Merton destroyed many of his writings, believing that his new life of denial would be one of exile from the world. Ironically, Merton believed that once he was received into the monastery, his writing would come to an end. Fortunately for us, Abbot Dom Frederic Dunne recognized Merton's gift for writing and requested the not-yet-thirty-year-old monk to write an account of his life and conversion.

Published in 1948, *The Seven Storey Mountain* became an instant best seller, was translated into multiple languages, and still today is readily available in bookstores in America, Europe, and Asia. One might say that Merton's writing career was launched at the same time as his monastic career. But Merton had much to learn in both arenas. In both writing and monasticism his inherited dualistic view was challenged. He soon discovered that the idea of the "four walls of my new freedom," celebrated in the concluding section of *The Seven Storey Mountain,* is paradoxically true (SSM 372). It is true that Merton exchanged his previously wild and undisciplined life of late-night drinking, jazz, and women for a more regulated lifestyle of prayer, labor, fasting, and mortification. But it is also true that Merton had yet to discover that God's love cannot be contained or restrained behind cloister walls, and that freedom involves not merely renunciation of past excesses, but an expanded vision—a new level of awareness, of being awake to embrace an entire universe.

Some of this transformation toward expanded vision appears early in Merton's journals. From a young academic who in 1941 wonders if he can love nature as a Trappist, Merton becomes a vowed member of the Order of Cistercians who, by 1948, has made peace with this wonderful gift from God. Seeds sown in childhood blossom into a new attitude that reveals a notable degree of integration of nature into his spirituality. For example, in his journal entry for the Feast of the Visitation, July 2, 1948, Merton describes not only the liturgical ceremony of Vigils the previous evening, but also the scenery beyond the refectory walls.

Since it was a fast day, we weren't long in the refectory in the evening, got out early and the sun was higher than it usually is in that
interval, and I saw the country in a light that we usually do not see.
The low-slanting rays picked out the foliage of the trees and highlighted a new wheatfield against the dark curtain of woods on the
knobs that were in shadow. It was very beautiful. Deep peace. Sheep
on the slopes behind the sheep barn. . . . I looked at all this in great
tranquility, with my soul and spirit quiet. For me landscape seems to
be important for contemplation . . . anyway, I have no scruples about
loving it. (ES 215–16)

No scruples about loving it. Landscape important for contemplation.
These two comments indicate that change—more precisely, a deepening awareness—is taking root in Merton. Some of his early contra-
dictory viewpoints are dissolving; the monastic ideal of unifying all
aspects of one's life is beginning to take hold in his evolving spiritual
consciousness. Moreover, what we notice about Merton's comment
here and in other journal entries is that he is not only *looking* at the
tranquility of nature, but also beginning to *recognize, respond to,* and
*articulate* the silence of the place. As the twentieth-century poet John
Moffitt phrases this challenge:

> To look at any thing . . . you must
> Be the thing you see . . . You must enter in
> To the small silences between
> The leaves,
> You must take your time
> And touch the very peace
> They issue from.[26]

Along with the challenge of integrating prayer, work, reading, and silence into a coherent monastic spirituality, Merton is allowing his early
childhood love of nature, as well as the monastery landscape, to be
a constructive force in shaping his imagination, entering into "small

silences between" and ultimately developing a sharply defined sense of place. And then, June 27, 1949: one small permission given by the abbot propels Merton into more exciting levels of awareness that not only transform and deepen his spiritual life, but also summon him to greater solitude and his final years in the hermitage.

## June 27, 1949—A Turning Point

By reading Merton's journals, one discovers that less than a year after admitting that landscape is important for contemplation, this monk is given permission to go beyond the confines of the cloister to walk and pray alone in the surrounding woods. As Jonathan Montaldo notes in *Entering the Silence,* one of the published volumes of Merton's journals, June 27 is a pivotal date in Merton's spiritual development. After this date the "expansiveness and depth" of Merton's prose "breaks out beyond a past mental and physical confinement" (ES 328n43). Readers of the journals will sense in Merton's writing a new "liberation, contentment, and heightened awareness" of his surroundings.[27]

Certainly the very length of the journal entry for June 27 indicates astonishing freedom and mounting excitement. Previous notations in Merton's journal extend for approximately half a page; this entry comprises five pages, and nothing else is written until July 10. One can reasonably presume that in the interim Merton was delighting in his novel possibilities for contemplation and exploring his new freedom *beyond* four walls. His June 27 journal entry offers a measure of validation for this conjecture. Previously, Merton had been commenting about the rain, his devotion at Mass, the composition of *Seeds of Contemplation,* a monastic visitation by the order's European superior, and—quite grumpily—the extra manual labor required even on feast days. Now, taken by surprise by this permission to pray outdoors beyond the cloister boundaries, Merton relishes his taste of new freedom: "And so I took advantage of it in the afternoon, although there was a wall of black sky beyond the knobs to the west, and you could hear thunder growling all the time in the distance. It was very hot and damp but there was a good wind coming from the direction of the storm." Merton then mentions how before chanting the office of None, he had dreamed of what it might be like in the new landscape, yet discovers the reality is even more satisfying. "First I stopped under an oak tree on top of the hill behind Nally's and sat there looking out at the wide sweep of the valley and the miles of flat woods over toward the straight-line of the horizon where Rohan's knob is. As soon as I get away from people the Presence of God invades me. And when I am not divided by being with strangers (in a sense anyone I live with will always remain a stranger), I am with Christ" (ES 328).

Invaded by God? Quite a startling metaphor, yet one that captures the intensity of his spiritual experience and the risk of transformation. After some reflection about how he often feels lonely in the midst of people, but never lonely when he is literally alone, Merton resumes describing the landscape and, in particular, the monastery from this new geographic perspective, which gives him an expanded sense of place. "Gethsemani looked beautiful from the hill. It made much more sense in its surroundings. We do not realize our own setting and we ought to: it is important to know where you are put on the face of the earth" (ES 329). Merton continues rhapsodizing about this geography he regards as an overwhelming gift:

> If we only knew how to *use* this space and this area of sky and these free woods. . . . But this place was simply wonderful. It was quiet as the Garden of Eden. I sat on the high bank, under young pines, and looked out over this glen. Right under me was a dry creek, with clean pools lying like glass between the shale pavement of the stream, and the shale was as white and crumpled as sea-biscuit. Down in the glen were the songs of marvelous birds. I saw the gold-orange flame of an oriole in a tree. Orioles are too shy to come near the monastery. There was a cardinal whistling somewhere, but the best song was that of two birds that sounded as wonderfully as nightingales and their song echoed through the wood. I could not tell what they were. I had never heard such birds before. The echo made the place sound more remote and self-contained, more perfectly enclosed, and more like Eden. And I thought—"Nobody ever comes here!" The marvelous quiet! The sweet scent of the woods—the clean stream, the peace, the inviolate solitude! And to think that no one pays any attention to it. (ES 329)

Using polysyndeton, the effective rhetorical device of multiple "ands" to underscore his distaste for *not* seeing the amazing beauty of the landscape, Merton laments, "It is there and we despise it, and we never taste anything like it with our fuss and our books and our sign-language and our tractors and our broken-down choir" (ES 329). Instead, his ability to go beyond mere looking, to really *see* his environment with a loving, contemplative gaze, transforms this outward glance into an inward glance and recognition of grace: "Everything inside me was swamped in a prayer that could not be quite pure because there was necessarily so much natural exultation. . . . To say I was happy is to say how far short the prayer was of perfection, but I was consciously and definitely and swimmingly happy, and I wonder how I ever stayed on the ground at all. The black clouds meanwhile piled up over the glen" (ES 330).

Returning to the monastery for Vespers through a "screen of woods," Merton experiences a profound spiritual insight: "One thing I must say: both in the wood and especially on my way back, crossing an open hillock, all that I had tasted in solitude seemed to have a luminously intelligible connection with the Mass . . . my prayer in the wood was eminently the prayer of a priest. . . . Could I end up as something of a hermit-priest, of a priest of the woods or the deserts or the hills, devoted to a Mass of pure adoration that would put all nature on my paten in the morning and praise God more explicitly with the birds?" (ES 331). Despite another mention of his desire for more solitude as a Carthusian, Merton concludes this lengthy journal entry with a sincere prayer: "Sacred Heart, give me the humility to see this and use your graces to be satisfied. Teach me to let *You* [underlined twice] sanctify me, and do not let me spoil it by trying to change all *Your* [underlined twice] plans with my own stupid ideas and feelings" (ES 332).

This long and poignant journal entry illustrates how Merton builds on his early contact with color, shapes, and sounds and allows the power of landscape to access and influence his inner landscape. Merton, having gained a father figure in the abbot and a spiritual family in the Trappist community—poignantly missing from his early life—finds that roaming in the woods and the uncultivated land beyond the cloister creates yet another sacred place that enlarges his imagination, stretches his consciousness, and invites him into deeper awareness and contemplation. The monastery grounds become, in one sense, another Prades in which to celebrate "Oh Sun! Oh joli!"; another Saint-Antonin, its "landscape, unified by the church and its heavenward spire"; another Murat and Rome, with wild woods and invitations to spiritual homecoming. Indeed, the woods and outlying territory of the monastery seem to offer Merton a geographic and emotional stability he had been longing for all his life. His deep-seated *longing* was being transformed into a deeply felt sense of *belonging*. How else to explain his elated disclosure a little more than a decade later in the hermitage he named St. Mary of Carmel: "The pines are tall and not low. There is frankly a house, demanding not attachment but responsibility. A silence for dedication and not for escape. Lit candles in the dusk. *Haec requies mea in saeculum saeculi* [This is my resting place forever]—the sense of a journey ended, of wandering at an end. *The first time in my life* I ever really felt I had come home and that my waiting and looking were ended" (TTW 79–80). How else to unlock the profound wisdom of his comment from the early 1960s as elaborated in *Conjectures*: "I belong to this parcel of land with rocky rills around it, with pine trees on it. These are the woods and fields that I have worked in, and walked in, and in which I have encountered the deepest mystery of my own life. And in a sense I never chose this place for myself, it was chosen for me" (CGB 257).

June 27, 1949, also represents the abbot's wise recognition of Merton's need to be in nature, his recognition of the potential for deeper prayer that contact with wilderness can stimulate, and an official invitation to savor a new awareness of both outer and inner landscapes. Indeed, two incidents in nature, recorded in Merton's journals in early 1950, and one reflective experience of the dawn birds in the 1960s, reworked for *Conjectures of a Guilty Bystander*, merit expanded discussion because they aptly illustrate how the habit of awareness—of really *seeing*—and the ability to respond to a graced moment transform and deepen Merton's spirituality.

*Chapter 3*

# "Spots of Time"
## Moments of Awakening

Sometimes we see a kind of truth all at once, in a flash, in a
whole.

—Thomas Merton, Columbia University class notes

Though we credit Merton's study of the visionary William Blake with
significant influence on his ability to appreciate art and to see differently, other literary influences on Merton's thinking and spiritual practice warrant examination, namely his academic encounter with William
Wordsworth. Although he never engaged in a sustained inquiry into
Wordsworth's writing, Merton's 1938 college class notes and later his
St. Bonaventure lecture notes bear testimony to an ongoing fascination with this British Romantic poet. Elsewhere I have written more
extensively about the biographical and literary resonance between
Merton and Wordsworth.[1] Suffice it here to acknowledge that Merton
had a love-hate relationship with William Wordsworth.

During two weeks of December 1940, for example, Merton fluc-
tuates between "believing Wordsworth a madman" and admitting in
his journal that "perhaps for the first time I am beginning to understand Wordsworth" (RM 271, 279). But in his 1938 Columbia University class notes from a course entitled "The Art of Poetry," Merton
scribbled this marginalia about Wordsworth's commitment to see more
acutely and more deeply: "Vision: Seeing what otherwise would not
be seen. Claims to see more than others because he takes the trouble

to look. . . . Vision so highly specialized it has now become prophetic. For W, a prophet definitely, a 'seer' . . . he has learned to see not appearances, but 'what is really there.'"[2]

Taking the trouble to look. Seeing what is really there. This process of focused awareness, of enhanced consciousness, is the backdrop for Wordsworth's famous lyrical passage on "spots of time" in book 12 of his epic-length autobiographical poem, *The Prelude: Growth of the Poet's Mind*.[3] Throughout this poem Wordsworth creates stunning descriptions of how memory and imagination frequently interact to create an opening-out of consciousness, what the Romantic poets called an experience of the "sublime" and what we might identify as an "epiphany." The salient phrases from this passage on "spots of time" from the 1850 edition of Wordsworth's poem are revealing.

> There are in our existence spots of time,
> That with distinct pre-eminence retain
> A renovating virtue, whence, . . .
> our minds
> Are nourished and invisibly repaired;
> A virtue, by which pleasure is enhanced,
> That penetrates, enables us to mount,
> When high, more high, and lifts us up when fallen.
> This efficacious spirit chiefly lurks
> Among those passages of life that give
> Profoundest knowledge to what point, and how,
> The mind is lord and master. . . .
> Such moments
> Are scattered everywhere, taking their date
> From our first childhood (book 12, lines 208–25)

Spots of time: a curious phrase that fuses time and place into one intense, intimate explosion of awareness. These paradoxical experiences are both "places when" and "times where" the intense power of the moment unleashes the imagination—Wordsworth's name for our highest spiritual faculty. According to the poet, these highly charged events contain a "renovating virtue" by which we are "nourished and invisibly repaired." The experience may have any of several results: it enhances pleasure, penetrates to our core, enables us to climb higher, or lifts us up when fallen. There is no guarantee that such an epiphany will occur; nevertheless, the potential for such experience is always present because an "efficacious spirit" lurks within and around us. *Seeing*—and recognizing—these "places when" and "times where" is essential to an intellectual and spiritual transformation that can result in expanded consciousness.

Not surprisingly, Merton offers a similar reflection on such moments of expanded consciousness in his journal entry for April 9, 1941—during his Holy Week retreat at Gethsemani before his official December 10 entrance into the monastery. He writes:

> Sometimes we see a kind of truth all at once, in a flash, in a whole. We grasp this truth at once, in its wholeness, as a block, but not in all its details. We see the whole perspective of its meaning at once, and easily. We get a vast, large, pleasing, happy general view of some truth that's near to us. We contemplate it a while, from this standpoint—as long as the truth stands vividly before us: we hold this new, luminous whole figure of truth in our minds—we do not understand it thoroughly by any means, but anyway we possess it to some extent, and with a kind of certain knowledge. (RM 338–39)

Theologians and spiritual directors might refer to spots of time or flashes of "truth at once, in its wholeness" as *kairos* moments, after which nothing about life or our understanding of it is the same; these events are so transforming they become right-angled occurrences that redirect the path of life. Psychologists might label them touchstone experiences that take root in a personality and become a yardstick by which the validity of subsequent events and experiences is measured. Linguistic labels aside, such deep experiences become spiritual surprises that nourish, repair, lift up, and enhance the soul intent on discovering God as the ground of its being. They become seeds sown in holy ground that germinate and erupt into spiritual insight, challenge, and affirmation precisely because the individual is alert to the action

50

of God. A spot of time, that is, a deeply felt spiritual insight or graced moment, demands taking off one's shoes in humble reverence because "the place whereon you stand is holy" (Exodus 3:5). In the words of Merton's marginalia, the experience is "seeing what otherwise would not be seen," seeing "not appearances, but 'what is really there.'" The key to the seeing and comprehending the depth, breadth, and significance of such an experience is being awake.

Merton demonstrates this ability to *see* multiple times in his life, but perhaps most poignantly in his last days as he approaches the great buddhas at Polonnaruwa. He is keenly aware of the "rain," the "mustachioed guide," the "wet grass," "wet sand," "silence," and the "great smiles" that create the precondition for an overwhelming experience of the ultimate unity of all things. Details recorded in *The Asian Journal* testify to Merton's epiphanic moment of "primal awareness" when he feels, "almost forcibly, jerked clean out of the habitual, half-tied vision of things, and an inner clearness, clarity, as if exploding from the rocks themselves, became evident and obvious" (AJ 231–35). To echo Wordsworth again, the "renovating virtue . . . / That penetrates" enables Merton to "mount / When high, more high." In the words of Merton's college notes, this interaction with the giant buddhas reveals "a kind of truth all at once, in a flash, in a whole"; or as Merton explains in his December 5 journal entry: "I know and have seen what I was obscurely looking for. I don't know what else remains but I have now seen and have pierced through the surface and have got beyond the shadow and the disguise" (AJ 236).

Spots of time—moments of intense vision and awareness that root new and permanent understanding in the soul—are not restricted to Merton's penultimate experience of Reality at Polonnaruwa, or to his earlier Fourth and Walnut streets insight into his connectedness to all people. Indeed, in the woods, wandering in nature—especially after the pivotal day of June 27, 1949—Merton experiences frequent and deep moments of spiritual awakening that, when low, lift him up and, when high, enable him to mount higher. Particularly salient are two examples detailed in his journal that qualify as spots of time: New Year's Day 1950 and February 10 of that same year.

# New Year's Day 1950

In the midst of a raw winter downpour, Merton took one of the two communal raincoats from the pegs outside the monastery chapel and set off into the woods. Although he had not intended it, he found himself climbing one of the steepest knobs. Reaching the top, as he writes in his journal, "I found there was something terrible about the landscape. But it was marvelous. The completely unfamiliar aspect of the forest beyond our rampart unnerved me. It was as though I were in another country" (ES 393). Some inner voice speaks to him: "Now you are indeed alone. Be prepared to fight the devil." Merton is definitely on a quest. Alas, nothing happens. As in Elijah's experience, God does not always speak in the mighty wind and teeming rain, but in the silence of the quiet breeze. So, too, for Merton on this January day. Disappointed and believing he has been on a fruitless pursuit, that he has not been privileged to engage in some existential battle with the forces of evil, Merton descends the hill. During his arduous, wet walk down the slope, he experiences a Wordsworthian "gentle shock of mild surprise."[4] Merton writes: "Half way down, and in a place of comparative shelter, just before the pine trees begin, I found a bower God had prepared for me like Jonas' ivy. It had been designed especially for this moment. There was a tree stump, in an even place. It was dry and a small cedar arched over it, like a green tent, forming an alcove. There I sat in silence and loved the wind in the forest and listened for a good while to God" (ES 394).

A bower designed for him by God. Bower—a word in medieval literature associated with intimacy and nuptial rituals. For Merton on this New Year's Day, this bower and his subsequent communion with God epitomize a *kairos* moment that focuses and reaffirms his commitment to deeper contemplation. In this bower Merton experiences not only the sublime in nature but also a new moment of *seeing* that is equal to a spiritual awakening. The conclusion to this journal entry is equally revealing: "The peace of the woods steals over me when I am at prayer." Nature has provided not the backdrop but the vehicle of contemplation for Merton. In such intense moments of communion,

52

A Kentucky knob. (Photo by Thomas Merton)

matter and spirit reveal to Merton not a duality traceable to ancient
Greek philosophy, but an essential cosmic unity. Because he first sees
the bower, and then is aware of its potential for intimacy with God, we
might say that in this spot of time inner and outer landscapes merge.

## February 10, 1950

Six weeks later Merton has another significant spiritual awakening because of his ability to see "what is really there." While praying one
evening in the attic of the garden house that served as a quasi hermitage in those early days, Merton became aware of excitement among

the myriad starlings roosting and singing in the nearby trees. An eagle soaring overhead suddenly attacked a tree full of starlings. Merton writes, "Before he was near them, the whole cloud of them left the tree and avoided him and he came nowhere near them." When peace had returned and the starlings were moving about the ground, once more singing, "like lightning, it happened. . . . From behind the house and from over my roof, a hawk came down like a bullet, and shot straight into the middle of the starlings just as they were getting off the ground. They rose into the air and there was a slight scuffle on the ground as the hawk got his talons into the one bird he had nailed. It was a terrible and yet beautiful thing, that lightning flight, straight as an arrow, that killed the slowest starling." Merton tries to resume his prayer, but the hawk, enjoying his feast in the adjacent meadow, distracts him. Merton's thoughts turn to medieval falconry, Arabian princes, and the way some people love war. "But in the end," writes Merton—and this is the significance of this spot of time—"I think that hawk is to be studied by saints and contemplatives because he knows his business. I wish I knew my business as well as he does his" (ES 407–8).

In this common experience of seeing the food chain in action, Merton perceives a transformative lesson. Practice. Practice. Practice. That hawk had honed his hunting skill over weeks, months (years perhaps), and Merton's awe at the bird's focus is a poignant reminder of the need to hone his own skills of solitude and contemplation. This graced moment is more than an experience of nature chiding her child; rather, by *seeing* what is really there before him, Merton is moved to ruminate on the importance of this experience. He even addresses the hawk as a fellow artist, reveling in his craft. With subtle allusions to Gerard Manley Hopkins's poem "The Windhover," in which Hopkins confides that his "heart in hiding / Stirred for a bird,—the achieve of, the mastery of the thing!"[5] Merton celebrates this other raptor and confides in his journal: "I wonder if my admiration for you [the hawk] gives me an affinity for you, artist! I wonder if there will ever be something connatural between us, between your flight and my heart, stirred in hiding to serve Christ, as you, soldier, serve your nature. And God's love a thousand times more terrible! I am going back to the attic and the shovels and the broken window and the trains in the valley and the prayer of Jesus" (ES 408). Practice. Practice. Practice.

These two spots of time that nurture Merton's spiritual awakening are indicative of the power of nature to evoke prayer and effect ongoing spiritual growth. Moreover, these illustrations provide clues for understanding Merton's fascination with nature and his ability to see—be awake to—the spiritual lessons they impart. This brings us to a third poignant example that offers insight into Merton's response to spots of time and growth in spiritual richness.

## The Birds Ask: Is It Time to Be?

The scene is ten years later, June 5, 1960, the feast of Pentecost. Merton's desire for more silence and solitude has been temporarily satisfied. The abbot has granted Merton permission to pray in an abandoned toolshed he names St. Anne's. Merton has been ordained a priest for eleven years. He has published *Seeds of Contemplation, The Sign of Jonas, No Man Is an Island, Selected Poems,* and *Thoughts in Solitude,* the last drafted in summer afternoons within the confines of St. Anne's. Merton is currently proofreading the galleys for *Disputed Questions.* Plans are being discussed to build a simple structure for ecumenical dialogue, on a clearing known as Mount Olivet, a structure that, before the year is out, will become the hermitage Merton has so longed for. Merton will be allowed at first to pray there for extended periods, and then in August 1965 to move in permanently as a hermit. But for now Merton has often prayed alone in the novitiate or outside in the woods. His childhood talent for noticing everything is in full sway. On this great feast of the birth of the church, Merton not only delights in his solitude but also recounts at length in his journal his exuberant and joyful experience of the previous Thursday—discovering "the *full meaning* of lauds, said against the background of waking birds and sunrise." With jubilant lyricism, Merton details the process of dawn: "At 2:30—no sounds except sometimes a bullfrog. Some mornings, he says Om—some days he is silent. The sounds are not every day the same. The whippoorwill who begins his mysterious whoop about 3 o'clock is not always near. Sometimes, like today, he is very far away in Linton's woods or beyond. Sometimes he is close, on Mount Olivet. Yesterday there were two, but both in the distance" (TTW 7).

Such keen observation. Such a level of awareness, developed from lifelong habits of seeing and noticing details of his surroundings. Merton continues: "The first chirps of the waking birds—'*le point vierge* [the virgin point]' of the dawn, a moment of awe and inexpressible innocence, when the Father in silence opens their eyes and they speak to Him, wondering if it is time to 'be'? And He tells them 'Yes.' Then they one by one wake and begin to sing. First the catbirds and cardinals and some others I do not recognize. Later, song sparrows, wrens, etc. Last of all doves, crows" (TTW 7). This passage is worth savoring for its awesome yet innocent description. The birds ask the Father if it is time to be. Not: may I wake up and move around, but may I come into being? With profound clarity Merton has skillfully articulated the genesis of day, the moment of creation that is repeated daily all over our planet, indeed, at every moment as the Creator lovingly keeps us all in being.

On a basic level we can certainly agree that Merton is a good writer. A casual reader might be tempted to dismiss this account of dawn landscape as mere poetic whimsy or the rhapsodic gesture of a pen gone wild, but Merton is not finished. His next paragraph (which does not occur in the more detached version published a few years later in *Conjectures of a Guilty Bystander*) qualifies this experience as a spot of time. Merton is able to identify the intimate transformation of this spiritual awakening, the more intense dawn—and dawning—that is taking place in his inner landscape. He writes: "With my hair almost on end and the eyes of the soul wide open I am present, without knowing it at all, in this unspeakable Paradise, and I behold this secret, this wide open secret which is there for everyone, free, and no one pays any attention. . . . Not even monks, shut up under fluorescent lights and face to face with the big books and the black notes and with one another, perhaps no longer seeing or hearing anything in the course of festive Lauds" (TTW 7).

"With my hair almost on end. . . ." In fewer than one hundred words, most of them having Anglo-Saxon roots, Merton captures the essence of "going beyond the shadow and the disguise." He sketches for us the first glimmer of morning and how that physical light pierces the darkness of his soul. This dawn—and every dawn for Merton—becomes its own spot of time—a deep experience of spiritual nourishment that lifts him even higher. The external, awesome break of morning echoes the equally awesome, internal spiritual awakening to the secret lure of Paradise. With his hair standing on end, Merton is fully alive, enjoying unforgettable and deeply focused contemplation. Merton shares a similar insight and an invitation to readers two years later in *New Seeds of Contemplation,* in which he defines contemplation as "life itself, fully awake, fully active, fully aware that it is alive. It is spiritual wonder. It is spontaneous awe at the sacredness of life, of being . . . a kind of spiritual vision" (NSC 1).

We are privileged in volume 4 of Merton's journals to witness this awareness, this intense engagement with creation. Yet we must not overlook a tone of lament in his interpretive comment. Although this genesis event is repeated daily and open to everyone, only those who have eyes to see—really *see*—and ears to hear—really *hear*—can enter into the depths and richness of the moment. For the time being, however, Merton is alone in this all-absorbing communion, yet he realizes a spiritual lesson to help him regain perspective on his periodic desire to transfer to a more austere community with more opportunities for solitude. He writes: "Oh paradise of simplicity, self-awareness—and self-forgetfulness—liberty, peace. . . . In this I have realized how silly and unreal are my rebellions, and yet how unavoidable is the pressure and artificiality of certain situations which 'have to be' because they are officially sacrosanct. Yet there is no need to rebel, only to ask *mercy*. And to trust in mercy. Which is what I have not done" (TTW 7). Merton's dawn becomes a powerful spiritual lesson about the necessity of *seeing,* the centrality of focus, and the value of contemplation that uncovers the greatest grace of all: God's mercy.

Merton frequently returns to the theme of mercy, experienced often in spots of time, by which he is "nourished and visibly repaired." For example, at the end of the famous "Fire Watch" passage from July

4, 1952, published in *The Sign of Jonas,* Merton, looking in awe at the expanse of sky, hears the Voice of God in Paradise: *"What was vile has become precious. What is now precious was never vile. . . . What was cruel has become merciful. What is now merciful was never cruel. . . . Mercy within mercy within mercy. I have forgiven the universe without end, because I have never known sin"* (SJ 362; italics in original).

A decade later, after a prayer vigil in the novitiate chapel and a night of sleep at the hermitage, Merton awakens, strangely aware that he is *"happy.* Said the strange word 'happiness' and realized that it was there, not as an 'it' or object. It simply was. And I was that." Coming down to the monastery on that frosty December morning under the "multitude of stars above the bare branches of woods" and overwhelmed by the beauty of the moment, Merton again has a deep awareness of this gift of mercy. "I was suddenly hit, as it were, with the whole package of meaning of everything: that the immense mercy of God was upon me, that the Lord in infinite kindness had looked down on me and given me this vocation out of love, and that he had always intended this, and how foolish and trivial had been all my fears and twistings and desperation" (DWL 177–78). Having frequently read and meditated on the letter to the Ephesians that celebrates "God who is rich in mercy, because of the great love he had for us" (Ephesians 2:4), Merton now realizes in the depths of his being and amid the presence of stunning natural elements this "truth all at once, in a flash, in a whole."

## Le point vierge

Merton's dawn birds and their request to "be" warrant further examination. When Merton revises this passage for inclusion in *Conjectures of a Guilty Bystander,* he places it as the opening vignette in part 3, entitled "The Night Spirit and the Dawn Air"—a direct reference to Mencius (Meng Tzu), a fourth-century B.C.E. Chinese philosopher who, believing in the inherent goodness of humanity, advocated for the critical rhythm of rest and regeneration (CGB 131–32). In this version of *le point vierge,* the intimacy of the moment—the stark honesty

Light across the meadow. (Photo by Thomas Merton)

of Merton's hair standing on end—is omitted. As Merton explains in his preface to *Conjectures,* he is constructing his "personal vision of the world in the 1960s" by fitting passages together "in a spontaneous, informal philosophic scheme in such a way that they react upon each other" (CGB 5–6). Such construction and reconstruction alters the audience of the discourse. *Conjectures* focuses on the reader as the primary target of Merton's remarks—not his personal, intimate, and spiritual reaction to an event. Consequently, in this rendition of the June 5, 1960, journal passage, more detail is given to the slow procession of dawn and the awakening of the birds—possibly so that readers can transport themselves to the scene.

Merton's scenario, rephrased for publication, begins with an all-important call to alertness: "How the valley awakes." Herein lies a paradox. Does "how" mean Let me describe for you how this awesome transformation occurs? Or is it an exclamation: How awesome is this daily re-creation! Whichever linguistic meaning Merton intends, his scenario elicits emotional response from the reader. The bullfrog in the pond chanting his "Om" merits a second sentence of description: "Some nights he is in Samadhi; there is not even an 'Om.'" The whippoorwill's call is now described as "mysterious and uninterrupted." And Merton's original lament that others are not alert to this amazing event extends in this version beyond the monks, blinded by their fluorescent lights and large choir books. In *Conjectures,* each of us is indicted. We, the readers, are his audience, the ones missing the awesome and central, yet delicate and tender, action of God. We are the blind, Merton chides, with "lights on. Clocks ticking. Thermostats working. Stoves cooking. Electric shavers filling radios with static." This daily spot of time—with its potential to nourish, heal, lift up, even elate—is unfortunately ignored by us, too dull and inattentive to catch its deep import. "Here is an unspeakable secret," Merton confides, "paradise is all around us and we do not understand. . . . It is wide open. 'Wisdom,' cries the dawn deacon, but we do not attend" (CGB 131–32). In this later version of the breaking dawn, *we* stand exposed, duly chastised.

One consistent phrase, however, that appears in both the journal version and the published *Conjectures* is worth mining for its original significance and Merton's intent in retaining it, namely *le point vierge.* This French phrase can be traced ultimately to the Sufi mystics, by way of Merton's correspondence with Louis Massignon, a French scholar of Islam, yet cannot be satisfactorily translated.[6] English speakers usually take it to mean the virgin point, the cusp, or break of dawn, that awesome moment of transition between dark and light, night and day. We can also describe *le point vierge* as the moment of poise when anything is possible. In the world of Shakespeare, for example, midsummer's eve is such a virgin point, a moment of poise, when fairy magic can alter the expected rhythm of the world; similarly, in athletics, *le point vierge* for the competitive platform diver is the moment of poise when, balanced on her toes and envisioning the triple somersault with a half twist about to be performed, the diver and indeed the entire

crowd hold their collective breath for what will transpire; for the bas-
ketball star standing at the free throw line, it is that timeless pause
just before his fingers release the ball. When Merton uses the phrase
*le point vierge,* he is investing it not only with this meaning of "virgin
point," but also with what scripture scholars would refer to as multiple
levels of meaning—what we might call surplus meaning.[7]

Certainly, in the dawn passage in his journal and its revision in
*Conjectures,* Merton is intending to lyrically capture the mystery of
transformation and the magic of each day's creation. To have birds
daily asking the Father permission to "be" and to have them waking
up one by one paints a stunning picture of creation and re-creation—*le
point vierge*—the pregnant moment of poise and God's mercy that
surrounds us. But Merton intends more resonance, more layers of
meaning, to this phrase than simple lyricism. He is investing the phrase
with surplus meaning that becomes clearer in subsequent passages in
*Conjectures* and in the miniature vignette of his days in the hermitage,
written in 1965, entitled *Day of a Stranger.*

In *Conjectures,* a mere twenty-five pages after the dramatic opening scene of birds waking, yet still in the section devoted to "the night
spirit and the dawn air," Merton inserts an account of his spiritual
awakening at Fourth and Walnut in Louisville. This published version has the added imagery, not found in the original journal entry, of
people "all walking around shining like the sun" (CGB 157). As he expands the journal account of this epiphanic moment to reflect further
on its spiritual meaning and the discovery of his unity with each of the
pedestrians at that busy downtown intersection, Merton returns to the
phrase *le point vierge*—not this time indicating the cusp of dawn but
pertaining to the inner spark in each of us that is God. *Le point vierge*
is still the virgin point, the moment of poise, but it takes on surplus
meaning of major significance. Listen to Merton:

> Again, that expression, *le point vierge,* (I cannot translate it) comes
> in here. At the center of our being is a point of nothingness which
> is untouched by sin and by illusion, a point of pure truth, a point or
> spark which belongs entirely to God, which is never at our disposal,
> from which God disposes of our lives, which is inaccessible to the

fantasies of our own mind or the brutalities of our own will. This little point of nothingness and of *absolute poverty* is the pure glory of God in us. It is so to speak His name written in us, as our poverty, as our indigence, as our dependence, as our sonship. It is like a pure diamond, blazing with the invisible light of heaven. It is in every-body, and if we could see it we would see these billions of points of light coming together in the face and blaze of a sun that would make all the darkness and cruelty of life vanish completely. . . . I have no program for this seeing. It is only given. But the gate of heaven is everywhere. (CGB 158)

Another lyrical passage, but now the beauty and sharp imagery of *le point vierge,* the virgin point, is not just out there in nature; it is within each human being. Indeed, *le point vierge* is the moment of creation, that daily creation of the world and the second-by-second re-creation of our being, yet it is also the living presence of God within us. *Le point vierge* is both an event and a dwelling. For the birds *le point vierge* is their innocent awakening in response to the Father's ongoing impulse of love; for us *le point vierge* is also the sustaining spark of Divinity within that allows us to recognize our unity with each other and with God's Self. Merton's view is that if we saw ourselves as we really are, "shining like the sun," we would rejoice in the absolute poverty within because there—in that inner point of nothingness—we discover God. We discover our True Self in God. Merton, the *bystander,* sees the beauty, innocence, and free gift of the dawn, expressed intimately in the birds asking the Father if it is time to "be." Then they awaken one by one. Merton, the *guilty* bystander, committed to solitude and con-templation, experiences a related awakening: namely, that our inner, absolute poverty is also to be recognized, celebrated, and cherished because this is where we truly exist in God. This inner nothingness, "untouched by sin and by illusion," is, because of God's mercy, the hidden ground of Love. This inner nothingness, this *point vierge,* is our paradise and its gate is everywhere—if only we are aware.

How does Merton do it? How does Merton grasp such weighty theological insights and offer them to us in simple yet challenging pictures? Surely he can do it because he is a writer. Surely he can do it because he works at responding to grace by means of silence, solitude, and contemplation. But, just as surely, nature plays a part in the revelation of divine secrets. In the silence of the dawn, watching for the first sign of light, Merton sees not only the genesis of the day, but also his own inner genesis, which is always innocent and pure. When the birds say "yes" to the Father, they wake up; when Merton acknowledges the pure glory of God within, he says "yes" to a fuller and deeper level of prayer and transforming spiritual consciousness. Awakening to the presence of God within is responding to the generative power of the Creator to "be" in a new way. Awakening to an experience of that inner point of nothingness (*le point vierge*) is to understand in a new way how "with my hair almost on end and the eyes of the soul wide open I am present, without knowing it at all, in this unspeakable Paradise" (TTW 7).

## Day of a Stranger

Spiritual awakenings are such a deep and pervading theme in Thomas Merton's prayer and journaling that they function as a focal point in his 1965 description of his life in the hermitage. Published as *Day of a Stranger,* this journal section reveals how Merton lives in the woods "out of necessity," in a kind of "ecological balance" (DS 33). Each day is immersed in nature, increased awareness of mercy, and attention to the call to "be."

> I am out of bed at two-fifteen in the morning, when the night is darkest and most silent. I find myself in the primordial lostness of night, solitude, forest, peace, a mind awake in the dark, looking for a light, not totally reconciled to being out of bed. A light appears, and in the light an ikon. There is now in the large darkness a small room of radiance with psalms in it. The psalms grow up silently by themselves without effort like plants in this light which is favorable to them. The plants hold themselves up on stems which have a single consistency, that of mercy, or rather great mercy. *Magna misericor-*

*Oh my, yes!!*

*dia.* In the formlessness of night and silence a word then pronounces itself: Mercy. . . . The birds begin to wake. It will soon be dawn. (DS 43–45)

A few pages later, he writes: "It is necessary for me to see the first point of light which begins to be dawn. It is necessary to be present alone at the resurrection of Day, in the blank silence when the sun appears. In this completely neutral instant I receive from the Eastern woods, the tall oaks, the one word 'DAY,' which is never the same. It is never spoken in any known language" (DS 51).

What to make of yet another exuberant description of the breaking dawn, *le point vierge*? First, we must acknowledge Merton's love of and immersion in nature. Then, in the light of his use of the term twice in *Conjectures* and his obvious, but implied, reference to it in *Day of a Stranger*, we must recognize and concede the power of nature to inform his spiritual life. Merton's journals and published writing confirm that nature is a primary vehicle for experiencing the inner secrets of the Divine—for experiencing them deeply, profoundly, and with lasting effect. Dawn, *le point vierge*, and its accompanying gift of mercy signal not just another genesis moment at twenty-four-hour intervals, but the continuous revelation of the Divine in the unfolding of the universe. Merton's love of color, landscape, creatures, stars, dawn nourishes his contemplation of this unfolding; all aspects of nature enable him frequently and deeply to go "beyond the shadow and the disguise." Indeed, as Merton's awareness of external landscape intensifies, his awareness and exploration of his internal landscape also intensifies. And in that inner landscape there is room to embrace issues of social justice, nonviolence, dialogue between East and West, Buddhism, and Islam.

Finding God in creatures is not, as Merton first believed, merely a stepping stone to God, but rather a bursting forth, an ongoing encounter with the Divine. Once he discovers how "landscape is important for contemplation," once he is permitted to wander in the woods, along the lakes, and on the knobs beyond the confines of the enclosure, Merton's capacity for contemplation expands. Each foray into nature, occasionally accompanied by a sudden and profound spiritual insight, is an invitation to discover more deeply his vocation. As he declares in an August 12, 1965, journal entry, "Our very creation itself is a beginning of revelation. Making us in His image, God reveals Himself to us, we are already His words to ourselves! Our very creation itself is a vocation to union with Him and our life, and in the world around us, if we persist in honesty and simplicity, cannot help speaking of Him and of our calling" (DWL 279).

Merton could not be more clear: our creation is itself a vocation to union with God—an ongoing call to wake up and ask the Father if it is time to "be." And though moments of spiritual revelation—spots of time—can jump-start our spiritual batteries, being awake enables us to experience the nourishment of contemplation: to become "life itself, fully awake, fully active, fully aware that it is alive" (NSC 1). Indeed, developing a habit of being awake so that we can incorporate signifi-cant touchstone moments into our lives invites us into the playfulness of Divinity itself.

Merton's final chapter in *New Seeds of Contemplation* neatly cap-tures the challenge of this reality. Genesis is a "poetic and symbolic rev-elation, a completely *true,* though not literal, revelation of God's view of the universe . . . a garden in which He himself took delight." Steep-ing himself in incarnational theology that is rooted in the holiness of matter, Merton celebrates a God not only enjoying creation, but also inviting human beings to be *homo faber,* stewards of the garden. Mer-ton's God is a model of self-emptying for his creatures, a paradox of the Pantokrator (all-powerful One), who is also the "hidden one, un-known, unremarkable, vulnerable," desiring union with humanity and inviting us to "forget ourselves on purpose, cast our awful solemnity to the winds and join in the general dance" (NSC 290–97). As he urges Latin American writers two years later in his "Message to Poets," it is necessary to feel the immediacy of "water on [one's] skin." Therefore, "Come dervishes: here is the water of life. Dance in it" (RU 161).

# Chapter 4

# Seeing Differently
## Recognizing the Holy in the Ordinary

> I myself am part of the weather and part of the climate and part of the place.
> —Thomas Merton, *Turning toward the World*

Though it is exciting and perhaps even clever to identify spots of time in a writer's life and thus infer or speculate on how singular events play a significant role in artistic or spiritual development, not everyone is a celebrity subject to such scrutiny. Yet all of us *do* have the opportunity to develop a new way of *seeing*, even to develop a habit of awareness that prepares us for contemplation and that allows us to reflect on ordinary events and times in our lives that subtly influence our thinking and recognition of the Divine. Certainly the Christian liturgical calendar, with its cycles of festivals and celebrations, supports this form of reflection. As I mentioned in chapter 2, Christians during Advent are invited to respond to the great call to awake in order to prepare for celebrating the mystery of Incarnation; subsequently, they are invited to a long, reflective Lent, as well as to rejoice during the fifty days of the Easter season, which culminate in the feast of Pentecost. Nevertheless, the rest of the liturgical calendar, though sprinkled with feast days of saints, is devoted to what the Christian church calls ordinary time.

Too often we think of ordinary time as mundane, commonplace, time in between, time in the idle mode when nothing happens. In reality, ordinary time is when multiple opportunities of grace and vision are offered to those who, like the virgins awaiting the delayed bridegroom, are awake and alert (Matthew 25:1–13). The paradox of ordinary time echoes the great paradoxes of Christianity: the first shall be last; one must lose one's life in order to gain it; the seed must fall into the ground and die in order to bear fruit; Good Friday must precede Easter Sunday. Ordinary elements of nature such as wheat, grapes, mustard seeds, and sheep are fodder for parables about the kingdom, as well as an invitation to recognize God's unconditional, outrageous love and to participate in Divine Life. Incarnation itself, a core doctrine of Christianity, declares loudly and unequivocally how God has transformed ordinary flesh and blood into the God-Man. Living in ordinary time, that is, *really* living each moment, affords one the leisure of being aware of ongoing activity, of *seeing* and recognizing the "meddling" of the Divine One, whose uncontainable love brings humanity into being and who sustains each individual at every moment. Rainer Maria Rilke, one of Merton's favorite poets, never tired of reminding readers that humans have the capacity to see the holy in the ordinary.[1] The sociologist Andrew Greeley maintains that "Catholics live in an enchanted world . . . haunted by a sense that the objects, events, and persons of daily life are revelations of grace."[2] An attitude of being aware of the "now" moment, of being alert to the Spirit-infused atmosphere in which individuals "live and move and have our being" (Acts 17:28) invites believers to revel in being connected to God, to discover and live the paradox of how *everyday* grace surrounds them *every day*.

Thus, it is important to examine not only the significant spiritual experiences in Thomas Merton's life, often triggered by some poignant soul-stretching interaction with nature, but also his day-to-day experience of nature. Such ongoing interaction of being awake to the now moment predisposes him to encounter the holy in the ordinary. Central to forming Merton's deepening habit of awareness and expanded consciousness is the ancient monastic tradition of chanting the Hebrew psalms. As Merton explains in his 1953 book on the psalms, each monk is challenged to "live on the psalms," for they are the "nourishment of his interior life and form the material of his meditations and of his own personal prayer, so that at last he comes to live them and experience them as if they were his own songs, his own prayers . . . They are bread, miraculously provided by Christ, to feed those who have followed Him into the wilderness."[3] According to the monastic *horarium,* Merton seven times a day sang praise to God, praise often cast in nature metaphors: a God who feeds us with the finest of the wheat (Psalm 81), who leads us to green pastures (Psalm 23), for whom even the sparrow finds a home and the swallow a nest (Psalm 84); a God who makes springs gush forth in the valley (Psalm 104), about whom the psalmist is moved to exclaim: "Let everything that has breath praise the Lord" (Psalm 150). Over the course of a week, all 150 psalms are chanted. Multiply that by months and years, and this poetry of praise becomes ingrained in a monk's interior life. Rhythmic phrases rise easily to his lips. As Merton comments in the mid-1960s: "The Psalms then are the purest expression of the essence of life in this universe . . . *cantate, jubilate, exultate* [sing, rejoice, exult]" (CGB 135–36).

Mircea Eliade, a historian of comparative religion, has pointed out that ritual or repeated action allows the transcendent beyond us to be experienced as the immanent within us. Ritual actually predisposes us to encounter the holy, to discover the holiness of the ordinary; repetition raises our awareness and puts us in touch with a remembrance of the original sacred moment.[4] In the opening lines of his 1949 poem "A Psalm," Merton lyrically expresses this ongoing transformation:

When psalms surprise me with their music
And antiphons turn to rum
The Spirit sings; the bottom drops out of my soul.

The result?

New eyes awaken . . .
And I am drunk with the great wilderness
Of the sixth day in Genesis. (CP 220–21)

In addition to regularly praying the psalms and steeping himself in the writings of the Fathers and Doctors of the Church such as Augustine, Thomas Aquinas, and Bernard, Merton studied the medieval mystics. He read, for example, Meister Eckhart, who extols the creative juiciness of God and treasures the divine spark residing within us; Hildegard of Bingen, who counsels us to become a feather on the breath of God; and Julian of Norwich, who celebrates a maternal God of ongoing birthing. Thus, in communal ritual and in private meditation Merton was discovering the immanence of the Divine, that is, we might say, the Energy of the present moment. He was experiencing the power and intensity of the ordinary that is apparent to those who *see* with new eyes.

Merton's scheduled times of private prayer often included roaming the monastery grounds. Once he is given permission to wander beyond the cloistered areas for daily meditation periods, his journal references to nature increase in number and in depth, offering ample evidence of how deeply the nature he experiences daily is influencing his writing and his prayer. For example, in the first section of Merton's monastic journals (volume 2, The Novitiate, December 1941–April 1942) there are three references to nature in his prose as well as mentions of earth, flowers, sun, hills, and the like in the several poems he includes; in the memoir dedicated to Dom Frederic Dunne (October 1946–August 1948) nature is mentioned twice. In the major portion of his journal, entitled "The Whale and the Ivy" (December 1946–July 1952), which covers this transition time before and after Merton was allowed free rein to pray outside the monastery cloister, there are 180 separate entries that refer to and celebrate nature. This section—later revised and published as *The Sign of Jonas*—ends with the rhapsodic and oft-quoted "Fire Watch" passage, in which Merton applauds the natural and spiritual rhythms of the night, with its "huge chorus of living beings . . . life singing in the watercourses, throbbing in the creeks and the fields and the trees, choirs of millions and millions of jumping and flying and creeping things. And far above me the cool sky opens upon the frozen distance of the stars" (ES 486).

By volume 5 of Merton's journals, the references to nature increase dramatically. *Dancing in the Water of Life*, which details his gradual move to the hermitage full-time, includes 225 separate entries about nature, not counting the four full pages that constitute the core

Trees silhouetted against the sky. (Photo by Thomas Merton)

of *Day of a Stranger,* first published in the Venezuelan journal *Papales.*[5] Throughout volume 5, the reader discovers just how significant nature is becoming to Merton's thinking and praying. Early on, he admits: "I am inevitably a dialogue with my surroundings" (DWL 48). Almost a year later he acknowledges, "I 'live' according to a different and more real tempo, live with the tempo of the sun and of the day, in harmony with what is around me" (DWL 146). Sunrise holds a particular attraction for Merton. He often celebrates the cusp of dawn, finding that his attention is "absorbed by the great arc of the sky and the trees and hills and grass and all things in them." He rejoices in the "enormous yolk of energy spreading and spreading as if to take over the sky. After that the ceremonies of birds feeding in the dewy grass, and the meadow-lark feeding and singing. Then the quiet, totally silent, day, warm mid morning under the climbing sun" (TTW 312). When Merton comes to revise this passage for *Conjectures,* he feels compelled to add to this catalogue of awakening: "April is not the cruelest month. Not in Kentucky" (CGB 294).

Being in the woods and having ordinary experiences of nature entwined with the rhythm of the day affirms Merton's vocation, and his journal entries give voice to the inner transformations subtly taking place. It is on one of these early mornings at dawn, as he is walking toward the monastery after an overnight at the hermitage, that Merton realizes how happy he is, and is "suddenly hit, as it were, with the whole package of meaning of everything: that the immense mercy of God was upon me, that the Lord in infinite kindness had looked down on me and given me this vocation out of love" (DWL 177–78). This kind of ongoing interaction with the ordinary generates another revealing journal entry a few months later: "There is no question for me that my one job as monk is to live the hermit life in simple direct contact with nature, primitively, quietly, doing some writing, maintaining such contacts as are willed by God, and bearing witness to the value and goodness of simple things and ways, and loving God in it all" (DWL 229).

How wonderful to have this Emersonian "savings bank of thoughts" in which we can see the growing influence of nature on Merton's thought, prayer, theology, and inner peace. How enchanting to share Merton's verbal landscapes, which reflect his artistic view of the ordinary geography surrounding him. The practice of being outdoors—perhaps subtly reminiscent of his infancy spent in the French sunlight while his father painted landscapes—creates for Merton a kind of symbolic homecoming. Reveling in nature brings Merton to a higher level of awareness in tune with the Divine; it allows him, in Greeley's words, "to sense grace lurking everywhere"[6] and consecrates ordinary time as an occasion of encounter with the Holy. In all, there are close to 1,800 nature references in the corpus of Merton's journals, the majority in entries after June 27, 1949. A sustained reading of his journals reveals his excitement about what he sees when meandering through the woods and climbing the knobs and illustrates how essential nature is to his thinking and praying. Like the twentieth-century Canadian painter Emily Carr, Merton understands that "God breathes in the forest."[7] Indeed, Merton's experiences in the woods as he looks at nature become, in William Blake's words, a moment of seeing "a world in a grain of sand,/and a heaven in a wild flower."[8]

I want to suggest that these increasingly frequent notations about nature throughout Merton's journals can be loosely arranged into four somewhat overlapping clusters: the *poetic eye* that sees and celebrates the uniqueness of creation; extended *metaphors* that probe and attempt to explain the conundrums of life; *weather reports* that offer insight into both external and internal atmospheres; and the frequent merging of *inner and outer landscapes,* landscapes that mediate and to some degree articulate Merton's ineffable experience of prayer. All these experiences of immersion in nature create the foundation for Merton's evolution toward a new level of responsibility for the welfare of nature and his development of an ecological consciousness. Let's examine each of these clusters or categories.

## The Poetic Eye

Merton always thought of himself as a poet, and he approaches the world with an artistic eye. His more than five hundred poems, collected in one volume and posthumously published in 1977, attest to his vocation as a writer. Merton did not merely dabble in words in either his poetry or his multiple essays and books; throughout his life he was committed to his craft—beginning with "Ermine Street," his first published poem in the *Oakhamian,* his high school newspaper. Recent discoveries of new poems, which the scholar Lynn Szabo calls "fugitive poems," continue to enlarge the Merton canon and challenge scholars to ongoing reevaluation of his literary talent.[9] Having won the literary prize at Columbia University in 1939 for the "best example of English verse," and cited as a new voice "aware of the living present and all it may hold of pain and purpose," Merton feels launched on a literary career.[10] Early in his adult life, he publishes *Thirty Poems* (1944), selected by his professor and mentor Mark Van Doren, followed by *A Man in the Divided Sea* (1946), *Figures for an Apocalypse* (1948), *The Tears of the Blind Lions* (1949), and, later, *The Strange Islands* (1957) and *Emblems of a Season of Fury* (1963). In addition, Merton publishes individual poems in the *New Yorker, Poetry, Experimental Review, Partisan Review, Horizon,* and *Spirit*.[11] His reading taste includes a strong love for the writing of William Blake; literary kinship with Gerard Manley Hopkins; knowledge of contemporary British and American poets; devotion to the Persian poet Rumi, who daringly wrote of the strange ways of an immanent God; and a lifelong esteem for the poetry of Rainer Maria Rilke.

Although several collections of Merton's poetry have been published, a recent and carefully nuanced selection of his poems, edited by Lynn Szabo with a preface by Kathleen Norris, offers readers a thematic approach to Merton's best poetry that clearly illustrates Merton's gift for perception. Changing the metaphor of sensory apprehension, Norris comments in her preface that Merton's poems are the fruit of listening. Norris, herself a writer and Benedictine oblate, understands the monastic practice from Benedict's Rule of listening with the "ear of the heart." Norris perceptively comments, "The poet who is a monk lives in a way that intensifies this process, as a life pared down to its essentials encourages close attention to the resonant tones of scripture and the lighter notes of wind and birdsong."[12] Adding to this evaluation of Merton's poetic talent, Szabo believes that Merton's "single most important gift to his readers was his prophetic vocation to perceive and distinguish in his art the fundamental unity in the cosmos. His understanding of the 'hidden Wholeness' of all things is embedded in his apprehension of the transcendent in the immanent."[13] To borrow Dennis Patrick O'Hara's words describing Merton's gift of seeing the transcendent in the immanent, matter "throbs with the spirit of God," and each created being is a means by which God becomes present.[14]

Such perception and expression of this fusion of the transcendent-immanent, this "hidden Wholeness," require a poet's eye (and ear and

73

heart), that is, the ability to listen and to *see* differently. How else to explain these evocative lines from Merton's early days in the monastery tenderly describing the landscape after night office: "It is not yet the grey and frosty time / When barns ride out of the night like ships" (CP 108–9). Or the Trappist brothers working:

> Now all our saws sing holy sonnets in this world of timber
> Where oaks go off like guns, and fall like cataracts,
> Pouring their roar into the wood's green well. (CP 96)

How else to explain Merton's poignant lines of grief for his younger brother, John Paul, whose Royal Canadian bomber was shot down and lost at sea in 1943:

> The silence of Whose tears shall fall
> Like bells upon your alien tomb.
> Hear them and come: they call you home. (CP 35–36)

How else to explain more cheerful images such as "all the frogs along the creek / Chant in the moony waters to the Queen of Peace" (CP 116–18); or

> where blue heaven's fading fire last shines
> Reflected in the poplar's ripple,
> One little, wakeful bird
> Sings like a shower. (CP 41–42)

For Merton, a language aficionado who sees images in nature and has no scruples about using landscape for contemplation, beauty is not restricted to fleeting poetic lyricism. Beauty is everywhere. One does not have to read far into Merton's journals to discover his fascination with color, shape, and sound. He notes the many changes of the weather and is enchanted by a perching bird or soaring hawk, the strumming of tree frogs, and the graceful drape of a wildflower. Even when he does not use any complicated figure of speech, his alert attention to the landscape around him enables him to articulate the uniqueness of the experience with a fresh turn of phrase or new-minted imagery.

Certainly not all Merton sees is inscribed in his journals, yet the increasing number of references to nature indicates that he is more and more acutely aware of ordinary surroundings, and that his love of nature and times of contemplation intertwine. He seems compelled to record the poetry of the moment and articulate his distinct sense of place. Snippets appear everywhere, often without warning to the reader and frequently as an outgrowth of Merton's reflection on serious spiritual issues. His lyric touch is evident in short, moving descriptions, as well as in longer, rhapsodic tributes to the elements. What is common to these notations is that Merton sees not only the object in itself but also its relationship to its local surroundings and, indeed, to the cosmos. We might say that in looking at the microcosm, Merton discovers the exploding macrocosm and deep Mystery within. Capturing these moments in writing allows Merton to be a chanticleer, reminding himself (and, by extension, the reader) of the importance of *seeing,* of being aware and awake.

Dipping into volume 3 of the journals, for example, the reader can discover numerous poetic descriptions that could well be lines for a poem and that offer support for Barry Lopez's insistence that geography influences the imagination. Merton notices that "three crows . . . flew by in the sun with light flashing on their rubber wings (SS 14); "Thunder and rain during mixt [light breakfast]. Curtains of mist hanging over the Knobs, pigs garrulous in the lush wet grass and a dove in the cedar tree—Enough for a *Haiku?* (SS 67); "A red shouldered hawk wheels slowly over Newton's farm as if making his own special silence in the air—as if tracing out a circle of silence in the sky" (SS 181); "Lovely blue and mauve shadows on the snow and the indescribably delicate color of the sunlit patches of snow. All the life of color is in the snow and the sky" (SS 171). This same commitment to the poet's eye, delighting in creatures and the seasons, continues throughout subsequent volumes of the journals, for example: "An indigo bunting flies down and grasps the long, swinging stem of a tiger lily and reaches out, from them, to eat the dry seed on top of a stalk of grass. A Chinese painting!" (TTW 228); "Dead dry weather! The leaves tinkle like flakes of copper when the breeze passes over them. Haze" (DWL 26); "The hills in the south stand out sharp against the immaculate morning. Soon the sun will rise. In the most pure silence a pileated woodpecker drums on a loud tree and the solemn sound goes out through the clear halls of the forest" (LL 30). One could say with the late philosopher and poet John O'Donohue that, for Merton,

> each day is a holy place
> Where the eucharist of the ordinary happens
> Transforming our broken fragments
> Into an eternal continuity that keeps us.[15]

Readers may have noticed that all the passages quoted so far celebrate the uniqueness, the goodness, the sacramental aspect of nature, and they might legitimately ask: What about the horror of nature, the brutality of some species' mating rituals and eating habits? Doesn't Merton acknowledge the other, cruel side of "red tooth and claw"? This is precisely the position articulated by Czesław Miłosz, the Polish poet and writer with whom Merton began a ten-year correspondence in 1958. In a letter dated February 28, 1960, Miłosz chides Merton: "Every time you speak of Nature, it appears to you as soothing, rich in symbols, as a veil or a curtain. You do not pay much attention to torture and suffering in Nature" (CT 65). Merton's response to this critique is clear: while he admits to many resentments in his life, he insists:

> It is not resentment against nature, only against people, institutions and myself. . . . I am in complete and deep complicity with nature, or imagine I am: nature and I are very good friends, and console one another for the stupidity and the infamy of the human race and its civilization. We at least get along, I say to the trees, and though I am perfectly aware that the spider eats the fly, that the singing of the birds may perhaps have something to do with hatred or pain of which I know nothing, still I can't make much of it. Spiders have always eaten flies and I can shut it out of my consciousness without

guilt. . . . I don't find it in myself to generate any horror for nature or a feeling of evil in it. (CT 65–66)

Merton refuses to take a Manichean approach to nature possibly because his experience with nature has developed in him such a deep sense of belonging, a sense of home.

# Extended Metaphors

Yet it is not too much of a literary leap for Merton to use poetic nature imagery when he is responding to frustration over monastery rules or working his way through the expected conundrums of life. His poetic eye, which is a gift of perception, becomes a tool to express what he is seeing and feeling. Merton not only recognizes and captures the intensity of the moment, but often, through an extended metaphor or analogy, works out his frustration to arrive at some degree of peace. Perhaps the most touching metaphor is Merton's cry of "unfair" in the guise of a caged bird. After learning that a meeting of American abbots will take place at Gethsemani the next year (1964) and that he is expected to offer some conferences for these religious superiors, Merton vents his bitterness at not being allowed to do the same at other monasteries:

> When the canary is asked to sing, well, he is expected to sing merrily and with spontaneity. It is true that I have a nicer cage than any other canary in the Order. . . . But this upsets me so that I cannot sleep. . . . Today I feel hateful, and miserable, exhausted, and I would gladly die. Everyone can come and see me in my cage, and Dom James can modestly rejoice in the fact that he is in absolute control of a bird that everyone wants to hear sing. This is the way birds stop singing—at least those songs that everyone wants to hear because they are comforting and they declare that all things are good just as they are. One's song is forced at times to become scandalous and even incomprehensible. (TTW 320–21)

Mention must be made, also, of the extended metaphor of Jonas and the whale, used to describe Merton's ongoing struggle over his vow of stability. Throughout his revised and reorganized journal published as *The Sign of Jonas,* but especially in the last section of entries from October 1950 to June 1952, Merton faces a dilemma: should he remain a monk at Gethsemani, which was growing more crowded, in part because of the literary success of *The Seven Storey Mountain,* or should he seek more solitude elsewhere? (SJ 305–48). He resolves this phase of his dilemma, knowing that Merton-Jonas must be subservient to the will of God, that is, in the "belly of the whale," wherever it carries him (SJ 10). "Thus God has brought me to Kentucky where the people are, for the most part, singularly without inhibitions. This is the precise place He has chosen for my sanctification. Here I must revise all my own absurd plans, and take myself as I am, Gethsemani as it is, and America as it is—atomic bomb and all" (SJ 323). A few pages later, he laments the confusion of cherishing the whale and abandoning the swimming Jonas, whereas it is Jonas who must emerge "free, holy and walking on the shore" (SJ 341).

Not all of Merton's extended metaphors describe troubling moments. Some capture with precision the professional trials facing him, some provide insight into his spiritual challenges, and some invite the reader into the uncharted territory of contemplation. In January 1948, for example, after reading the proofs of *The Seven Storey Mountain,* Merton speaks of the need to cut eight thousand words from "this whole mass of stuff, this big, frowsy, disheveled tree that has to be pruned into some kind of order and fruitfulness. St. Paul, help me out, sharpen all my scissors!" (ES 160). Just before Passion Sunday 1949, Merton ponders the faults and imperfections that "grow out of me like weeds. Their leaves are waving all over me. They grow out of my hands like tobacco. And still I am not unhappy" (ES 296–97). About six months after becoming Master of Scholastics, Merton reflects on the burdens and challenges of forming young monks. Instead of finding this work distracting him from his desire for solitude, he discovers that he needs to develop a hermit heart in order to care for the spiritual life of these men. "What is my new desert? The name of it is *compassion.* There is no wilderness so terrible, so beautiful, so arid and so fruitful as the wilderness of compassion. It is the only desert that shall truly

78

flourish like the lily. It shall become a pool, it shall bud forth and blossom and rejoice with joy. It is the desert of compassion that the thirsty land turns into springs of water, that the poor possess all things" (ES 463). Merton's paradoxical insight is echoed and reinforced by Beldon Lane: to find oneself empty in the wilderness—lost at the end of the trail, without hope of return—and to be met there unexpectedly by grace is the soul's deepest longing. The place of death in the desert becomes the place of miraculous nourishment and hope.[16] Some years later, after he reads Guerric of Igny's fourth Advent sermon, the desert metaphor again offers Merton a vehicle to comment on the necessity of Christ's grace. "The desert is given us to get the evil unnested from the crannies of our own hearts. . . . After twenty-three years all the nests are well established. But in solitude and open air they are revealed and the wind blows on them and I know they must go!" (DWL 177). Pruning shears, waving weeds, blooming deserts, nests of imperfection—all vivid nature imagery invented by Merton's poetic eye to paint a precise and poignant picture, reminding him of the seriousness of each challenge.

Merton also uses water and sea imagery to explore his spiritual life and experience of prayer. A few entries after his description of the unwanted nests in his heart, Merton reflects on his fiftieth birthday. He delights in his attraction to Sophia/Wisdom and the privilege of occasional overnights in his hermitage—and he confides in his journal a new, deep insight into his vocation to solitude: "Last night, before going to bed, realized momentarily what solitude really means: When the ropes are cast off and the skiff is no longer tied to land, but heads out to sea without ties, without restraints! Not the sea of passion, on the contrary, the sea of purity and love that is without care" (DWL 200). Sea imagery may seem an ordinary and simple literary construct, but the metaphor of being far out at sea without a tether, without charts or view of land, with only the presence of God as guide, is monumental. It is probably safe to infer that Merton's experience of being separated from the routine noises in the monastery, of being alone in the wilderness, surrounded only by night critters foraging for food and early morning birds responding to the first glimmer of light, is a singular grace of the ordinary that allows him to perceive, as never before, his intimate and unique love relationship with God.

The sea, with it boundless waves and unimaginable depths, is also a viable metaphor for boundless and unimaginable depths of prayer. Trying to describe his experience of contemplation, Merton again resorts to water imagery. In February 1952, the day before Ash Wednesday, Merton is sitting in the sun, the "blue elm tree near at hand, and the light blue hills in the distance." But as he pauses "between direction and work . . . big blue and purple fish swim past me in the darkness of my empty mind, this sea which opens within me as soon as I close my eyes. Delightful darkness, delightful sun, shining on a world which, for all I care, has already ended. . . . The hills are as pure as jade in the distance. God is in His transparent world, but He is too sacred to be mentioned, too holy to be observed. I sit in silence. The big deep fish are purple in my sea" (ES 467).

Merton continues in this musing vein for two pages, metaphorically describing the deepening levels of his contemplation. At the first level is the "slightly troubled surface of the sea" where there are action, plans, and resolutions. When he closes his eyes to sink to the second level, "the big blue, purple, green, and gray fish swim by." He is immersed in a "water-cavern" that acts as a comforting womb of security and soundless place of rest. "In the depth of the waters, peace, peace, peace." At the third level is the great paradox of transcendent and immanent Divinity:

> positive life swimming in the rich darkness which is . . . pure, like air. Starlight, and you do not know where it is coming from. Moonlight is in this prayer, stillness, waiting for the Redeemer. . . . Everything is charged with intelligence, though all is night. . . . Everything is spirit. Here God is adored, His coming is recognized, He is received as soon as He is expected, and because He is expected, He is received, but He has passed by sooner than He arrived. He has gone before He came. He returned forever. He never yet passed by and already He had disappeared for all eternity. He is and He is not. Everything and Nothing. . . . This is the holy cellar of my mortal existence, which opens into the sky. (ES 468)

Merton closes this lengthy nature passage with perhaps his most exuberant and paradoxical expression of prayer: "It is a strange awakening to find the sky inside you and beneath you and above you and all around you so that your spirit is one with the sky, and all is positive night" (ES 468).

## "And Now for the Weather . . ."

As a writer and the son of artists, Merton is skilled in guiding his eye to first look at and then *see* landscape and objects in nature in ways a bit different from how others might. And though these nature images delight and inspire, a careful reader will quickly notice that Merton mentions weather intermittently throughout his journals. Indeed, weather is very much a part of the ordinary. It is the air we breathe and the breeze that cools us, the snow we shovel, raindrops we dodge or lift our faces to receive. It is the sunshine we bask in. Changeable as it is, weather announces itself daily—and in some geographic areas, according to wags and punsters, every fifteen minutes. Some of us are more sensitive to these changes than others; most of us note the differences, if not in writing, then in casual conversation with family, coworkers, even strangers at the bus stop or supermarket. As we read through Merton's journals, it would appear that he, too, is one of us marking the passage of days in the monastery with simple weather reports. Merton's frequent references to weather indicate something deeper, more significant to his developing spirituality, however: namely, his recognition and experience of the power of place and the unity of all creation. *depth of seeing searches*

At first glance, Merton's multiple references to light, the configuration of clouds over the distant knobs, and the frequent Kentucky rains seem commonplace, a chaotic collection of weather data. What look like ordinary weather reports appear at the beginning of entries, sometimes between two long discussions of events in the monastery or notes on his reading. Occasionally they provide the finale for his musings that day. These comments are usually straightforward: "All day it has been dark and hot and wet. Sweat rolls down your back in church" (ES 217); "Another of the beautiful, cool days we have been having all year. We did not work this afternoon" (ES 86); "Frost again. Yesterday—beautiful October weather" (DWL 302); "It is grey outside, and snow falls lightly" (ES 34); "Hot, murky afternoon" (TTW 229); "Light rain all night" (DWL 224); "Sound of rain in the night—I lay in bed appalled by the weight of water falling upon the earth, it seemed, in a solid mass. Wonder what happened to the crops" (SS 213); "There was more rain and cold wind. In the east there were storms" (TTW 121); "During the morning meditation there was a fine thundershower, shaking the whole monastery, floods of rain" (TTW 220); "Heavy rain, breaking up in the warm afternoon" (LL 48). Rain—because of the Kentucky climate and the quasi companionship it provides in the woods—seems to merit frequent comment.

Such commonplace annotations remind me of how my mother often began phone conversations or letters, or how occasionally today long-distance e-mail correspondence begins with a comment on the local weather conditions. Weather references resemble, too, the calendars or daybooks kept by midwestern farmers, recording weather data that shape their field activities for the day and provide, over time, a log of climatic patterns and community responses to them. These references are reminiscent of the written reflections of modern desert dwellers, such as Terry Tempest Williams, who writes compellingly about the "intensity of living in an episodic landscape where thunderstorms, flash floods, and wind break any threat of monotony."[17] Such weather reports resemble also the even older practice of marking seasonal changes, for example, the "bird song calendars" kept by medieval monks, like that of Pseudo Bede, which cites February 11 or 12 as the "day when the birds begin to sing."[18] Whatever the motivation and resemblance, such weather data supply a "setting of normalcy" for Merton. In some unconscious way, notes one Merton scholar, Ross Labrie, Merton is painting the whole canvas, so that his particular experience appears "natural" and "bearable."[19]

I sense there may be a yet stronger import to weather imagery emerging in Merton's writing: his weather notations are simultaneously background and foreground for his writing. They are background or context for his poetic eye because they feed his imagination and provide fodder for language; at the same time, they are foreground and impetus for his imaginative wanderings because they allow him to explore new relationships of unity between and among creatures. Indeed, references to weather influence Merton's thinking and spiritual development as much as they reflect it. Merton must have been aware of the power of weather early in his life, but not until five years before his death does he comment on the significance of being aware of this ordinary phenomenon. In his entry for Ash Wednesday 1963, Merton confides:

> Our mentioning of the weather . . . [is] perhaps not idle. Perhaps we have a deep and legitimate need to know in our entire being what the day is like, to *see* it and *feel* it, to know how the sky is grey, paler in the south, with patches of blue in the southwest, with snow on the ground, the thermometer at 18, and cold wind making your ears ache. I have a real need to know these things because I myself am part of the weather and part of the climate and part of the place, and a day in which I have not shared truly in all this is no day at all. It is certainly part of my life of prayer. (TTW 299–300)[20]

"I myself am part of the weather. . . . It is certainly part of my life of prayer." This is a profound admission that bears further examination. First, it should be noted that the practice of reading weather is not unique to this one Trappist monk. Many cultures pay attention to weather. Native Americans, for example, believe that weather is a natural phenomenon of contact with the "numinous."[21] Our early Puritan ancestors, adept at reading their Bibles, were just as adept at reading clouds and plowed fields. More recently, the nature writer Gretel Ehrlich has commented, "A person's life is not a series of dramatic events for which he or she is applauded or exiled but a slow accumulation of days, seasons, years . . . anchored by a land-bound sense of place."[22]

Merton seems to have begun his reflective practice of reading weather early in his monastic experience. In *The Seven Storey Mountain* he writes that by his entering the Trappist monastery, his physical journeying is over; as a monk, then, he is free to experience the knobs and valleys of the monastery property, note the mist or rain, sun or breeze, and their connection to the weather of his heart. We perceive some sense of a developing intimacy with the Kentucky weather and the landscape in Merton's early journals; we witness the validity and vitality of this perception particularly in entries after June 1949. For example, Merton recounts how essential the experience of dawn is to his prayer. On Holy Saturday, April 8, 1950, he writes: "The darkness is thinning and expects the sun. Birds begin to sing. No Mass. Everything is waiting for the Resurrection" (ES 428). Two years later, in June 1952, after distributing Communion to the Trappist Brothers at 3:00 A.M., Merton confides that he "kneel[s] in the dark behind the relic case next to Saint Malachy's altar, while the sky grows pale outside over the forest, and a little cool air seeps in through the slats of the broken shutters. The birds sing, and the crickets sing, and one priest is silent with God. As soon as the morning angelus rings, I go out into the new day, my own new private dawn, which belongs to me alone" (SJ 345).

A short time later, in *Thoughts in Solitude,* written in the outdoor seclusion of the monastery toolshed, Merton investigates and probes our shared call to awaken our whole being to the presence of God (TS 51). In one of the later sections of this collection of short meditations, he articulates the interface between his vocation and the landscape: "Vocation to Solitude—To deliver oneself up, to hand oneself over, entrust oneself completely to the silence of a wide landscape of woods and hills, or sea, or desert; to sit still while the sun comes up over that land and fills its silences with light" (TS 101).

Keen awareness of the weather—and by extension, the entire landscape—offers human beings an ongoing way of constructing and nurturing meaning in the world. Reading the weather and the landscape, Belden Lane argues, is integral to the process of "dwelling" in a place so as to make it one's own.[23] In Donald St. John's words, Merton "was actively involved in making Gethsemani a sacred place. A new geography was being discovered and created."[24] In his skillful reading of *The Sign of Jonas,* St. John maintains rightly that because Merton was an "inveterate traveler" sensitive to the new, deeper geography of Gethsemani, his journals become "guidebooks" to help Merton transform his monastic role from mere traveler to dweller.[25] As traveler, Merton would just be passing through this monastic experience on his way to something else, whatever that might be; as dweller, he would be anchored in an ever-deepening sense of place, understanding, as Lane does, that the "wildest, most dangerous trails are always the ones within."[26] Merton himself offers testimony to his transitioning into dweller. After the rhapsodic celebration of his own private dawn with "almost two hours to pray or read or think by myself," he affirms: "This is the land where you have given me roots in eternity, O God of heaven and earth. This is the burning promised land, the house of God, the gate of heaven, the place of peace, the place of silence, the place of wrestling with the angel" (SJ 345).

Merton's powerful admission a dozen years later continues to haunt me: "I myself am part of the weather and part of the climate and part of the place. . . . It is certainly part of my life of prayer." After reading several volumes of Merton's journals and sometimes skipping over the ubiquitous weather reports, I suddenly realized how profoundly weather had been shaping Merton's spirituality over the years. Comments about the weather were not *solely* idle interjections into richer journal entries. They were not *merely* linguistic exercises, but a way of expressing an integral part of his inner and outer life. Weather was not some "Other" to be enjoyed, ignored, or adapted to; rather, weather was somehow infused into Merton's being. For him, the Western split between subject and object had dissolved. His quasi-flippant remark in *Day of a Stranger*—"What I wear is pants. What I do is live. How I pray is breathe" (DS 41)—takes on even deeper meaning, revealing the playfulness and hope of the "desert eccentric" who, free from the tensions of a stifling city, understands the unifying experience of ordinariness.[27] Merton had discovered how all experience of the external world is connected to the internal world. Inner and outer terrains impinge on each other. If Merton's journals and notebooks are guidebooks, then weather reports provide more than a manual of where and when to go; more accurately, they point the way for Merton to explore a "deep geography in which the divine, human, and natural orders mutually revealed and dwelt in each other."[28] Indeed, the entirety of Merton's journals, weather reports included, are not a guide how to *act*, but a guide how to *be*. That is to say, *habitat*—the weather and, in reality, the whole landscape—are interlaced with *habitus*—Merton's way of living. As Belden Lane contends, "A carefully formed *habitus* offers the vision necessary for discovering the deepest meanings of one's habitat." The terrain "reveals its secrets to those who are attentive, who see with the eyes of a tradition molded by the land itself."[29]

Merton not only looks at weather—physically distinct from himself—but allows it inside him, to become part of his prayer. His outward glance at the clouds, the rain, the wind evolves into an inward reality so that he discovers the "sky inside [him]" and his "spirit is one with the sky" (ES 468). Weather, with its repetition and innate power, becomes a kind of liturgy, reaffirming its contribution to the creation and rhythmic celebration of the ordinary. Two additional perspectives on weather are worthy of comment: its ability to teach new truths about relationship, and its power to transcend dualistic thinking. Simply said, weather can be both classroom and sign of our essential unity.

## Weather as Classroom

Mary Austin, in her 1903 collection of essays, *The Land of Little Rain,* articulates forcefully the power of weather to teach important lessons. She notes that storms "have habits to be learned, appointed paths, seasons, and warnings, and they leave you in no doubt about their performances. . . . The effect of cloud study is a sense of presence and intention in storm processes. Weather does not happen. It is the visible manifestation of the Spirit moving itself in the void. It gathers itself together under the heavens; rains, snows, yearns mightily in wind, smiles."[30] What a wonderful description of the activity of the Spirit! Sadly, not everyone is aware of this cosmic classroom and its life-giving lessons. Near the end of her essay, Austin castigates the ironic inattention of the weather scientist who, because he never thinks beyond his instruments and mathematical calculations, cannot comprehend the meaning of his knowledge. Unaware, he misses the cosmic celebration beyond his office door. She writes, "The Weather Bureau, situated advantageously for that very business, taps the record on his instruments

View of the monastery from the hermitage path. (Photo by Thomas Merton)

and going out on the streets denies his God, not having gathered the sense of what he has seen."[31]

This indictment of meteorologists as mere technicians or clerks reporting something they suppose has no influence on any aspect of their lives contrasts markedly with Thomas Merton's commitment to understand the significance of weather on his physical and spiritual, his external and internal, well-being.

Although Merton did not have access to Austin's writing, he too understood that weather offers lessons. In his widely anthologized essay "Rain and the Rhinoceros" (1966), Merton celebrates the meaningful meaninglessness of rain (RU 9–23). Alone in his hermitage in the woods during a long evening of steady rain, he is aware of the all-encompassing power of rain to make itself heard on the porch, the roof, the trees—a veritable sacrament of the present moment. This weather pattern subsequently becomes both *background and ground* to Merton's reflection: it becomes both the impetus for his writing and the controlling image of his meditation on the distinction between apparent uselessness and functionality, that is, between *bonum* (that which is inherently good, but not practical) and *utilitas* (that which is practically good). Attuned to the "climate of woods," Merton declares rain to be a "festival." In the first paragraph he writes, "I celebrate its gratuity and its meaninglessness," and he then testifies to the importance of listening to "all that speech pouring down, selling nothing, judging nobody. . . . What a thing it is to sit absolutely alone, in the forest, at night, cherished by this wonderful, unintelligible, perfectly innocent speech, the most comforting speech in the world" (RU 9–10). How adept Merton is at not only listening to the Word of God in scripture but also, in true Benedictine tradition, listening with the eye of the heart to the profound scripture of nature. With the fourth-century Anthony of Egypt, Merton could say, "My book is the nature of created things; whenever I want to read the Word of God, it is always there before me."[32]

In contrast to his experience of communion with the rain's "enormous virginal myth, a whole world of meaning, of secrecy, of silence, of rumor," Merton reflects on how rain in the city is most often considered an inconvenience. Human beings, because they are not awake, because they are not attentive, have precluded themselves from seeing "that the streets shine beautifully, that they themselves are walking on stars and water" (RU 10–12). Just as Mary Austin learns lessons from weather, so does Merton learn lasting spiritual lessons from the rain tapping on the roof of his hermitage. Whereas Austin chides unreflective weather statisticians, Merton chides "city people [who] prefer a stubborn and fabricated dream . . . a world of mechanical fictions which contemn nature and seek only to use it up, thus preventing it from renewing itself and man" (RU 11). Nature's rhythms are what we should be learning, maintains Merton, not patterns crafted by an engineer. The lesson ordinary rain teaches is that we are always on holy ground.

Learning from weather, that is, "listening" as well as "seeing differently," allows Merton metaphorically to weather the storms of his vocation. Like the apostles in the storm-tossed boat on the Sea of Galilee (Mark 4:35–41), Merton periodically experiences his own spiritual tempests. When Merton imagines Jesus is asleep, he resorts to scheming and manipulation to actuate what he *thinks* is God's will for him. The torment ceases when Jesus is roused and commands the tempest: "Quiet! Be still!" In the 1940s and 1950s, for example, Merton believes he is called to deeper contemplation that can be supported only by joining the Carthusians or the Camaldolese. When requests for a transfer are refused and Merton is appointed Master of Scholastics and then Novice Master, the tempest subsides or at least is sublimated through his writing. As Patrick O'Connell notes, Merton is clearly experiencing "tension between his public role and his private yearnings," yet his pamphlets and books about monasticism during this period are both an "expression of his attraction toward other, more solitary forms of monasticism, and perhaps . . . a way of exorcising it, of entering into the Carthusian and Camaldolese life in a literary rather than a literal way."[33] Merton's journal entries reveal these tensions, but they also bear witness to how instrumental weather and landscape are in deepening his sense of place and regaining emotional stability. Intermittently he is able to say: "God has brought me to Kentucky . . . the precise place He has chosen for my sanctification" (SJ 323); "Today I have been overpowered by the realization of how much I love *these woods* (and this woodshed). . . . *Question*—After I have gone to the trouble of moving the world to go to Mexico, will I find there half of what already I possess in the woods here?" (SS 278).

## Weather as a Sign of Our Essential Unity

In the 1960s Merton would have had no way of knowing that almost forty years later literary scholars and philosophers would identify weather as a sign of the interdependence and unity of all things—a sign that contradicts the dualistic paradigm revered by eighteenth-century Enlightenment thinkers, namely, that human beings with their rational minds have the power to master the laws of nature and, in particular, weather. In Jonathan Bate's view, weather is a primary force and symbol for our essential interdependence. Bate writes: "Ecosystems evolve in time through the operation of weather; the ecology of the human mind is equally dependent on the two senses of *temps* [weather and clock time]. Our moods are affected by the weather. Our identities are constituted in both time and place, are always shaped by memory and environment."[34] In short, weather mediates between our interior and exterior landscapes or ecologies; weather signals how totally dependent we are on everything in our environment, how we are influenced by everything in nature around us, and how we are an integral part of a larger cosmic whole.

Peasants and sailors have always had a sense of the reciprocal intimacy between weather and human activity; and poets, perhaps more easily than theologians, can imagine beyond the limits of dualism to mythic wholeness. In Bate's view, the popularity of British Romantic poetry officially calls into question Descartes's theory of the supremacy of human reason over the elements. To illustrate his position, Bate points to the bleak despair in Lord Byron's poem "Darkness," written a year after the 1815 eruption of the volcano at Tambora in Indonesia.[35] Because volcanic dust from that eruption clotted the atmosphere, covered the sun, and lowered temperatures, most of Europe and many areas of the Americas suffered crop failure for the next three years. Bate argues that although Tambora is not specifically mentioned in Byron's poem, the poem is nevertheless motivated by the pervasive influence of a catastrophic weather event. In contrast to Byron's text, yet similar in influence, is John Keats's 1818 poem "To Autumn," offered by Bate as a celebration of the Earth healing itself—another example of the reciprocal influence of human imagination and nature.[36] Bate's point is that weather is not only outside us; it permeates our living and in no small measure influences human imagination and human behavior—a principle offered by Barry Lopez, Belden Lane, Donald St. John, and others, and a truth Merton was discovering in his own corner of Kentucky, with its awesome knobs and frequent rain.

Though Merton does not admit in writing until 1963 that "I myself am part of the weather and part of the climate and part of the place," we have several earlier hints of how deeply aspects of weather and nature are part of his spiritual ecology. Several months after Merton was allowed to roam the landscape beyond the cloister, he notes that his

> chief joy was to escape to the attic of the garden house and the little broken window that looks out over the valley. There in the silence I love the green grass. The tortured gestures of the apple trees have become part of my prayer. I look at the shining water under the willows and listen to the sweet songs of all the living things that are in our woods and fields. So much do I love this solitude that, when I walk out along the road to the old barns that stand alone, far from the new buildings, delight begins to overpower me from head to foot and peace smiles even in the marrow of my bones. (ES 419)

As further testimony to his commitment to being aware of the weather as a sign of the essential unity of all creation, recall the concluding statement to his metaphorical description of the depths of prayer—the swimming colorful fish and the sinking deeper into positive night—"It is a strange awakening to find the sky inside you and beneath you and above you" (ES 468). In *Thoughts in Solitude* Merton again attests to this intrinsic unity: "Let me seek, then, the gift of silence, and poverty, and solitude, where everything I touch is turned into prayer: where the sky is my prayer, the birds are my prayer, the wind in the trees is my prayer, for God is all in all" (TS 94).

It is one thing for a nature writer such as Barry Lopez to reveal the power of geography to influence imagination and the development of a person, and for Belden Lane and Donald St. John to discuss how external and internal terrains can transform a traveler into a dweller. It is perhaps more convincing testimony to discover in Merton's journals how frequent were his interactions with nature, how ordinary, yet how profoundly transforming. This kind of awareness of place and geography—habitat becoming ritual, habit, *habitus*—enables Merton to pen lyrical, provocative, and startling lines that are not mere verbal rhapsodizing. Rather, they illustrate how intensely nature is moving him toward an integrated inner and outer landscape. Because Merton believes this kind of spirituality and prayer is available to all, not just to vowed, cloistered monks, everyone who so chooses can engage in a process of finding the Divine Voice in the ordinary—if he or she is awake to the awesome unfolding of Love that continues since the moment of Creation. Silence, solitude, awareness are the necessary ingredients for this experience of unity—which deepens into communion. As Merton phrases it:

> When your tongue is silent, you can rest in the silence of the forest. When your imagination is silent, the forest speaks to you, tells you of its unreality and of the Reality of God. But when your mind is silent, then the forest suddenly becomes magnificently real and blazes transparently with the Reality of God. For now I know that the Creation, which first seems to reveal Him in concepts, then seems to hide Him by the same concepts, finally *is revealed in Him,* in the Holy Spirit. And we who are in God find ourselves united in Him with all that springs from Him. This is prayer, and this is glory! (ES 471)

# Chapter 5

# Merging Inner and Outer Landscapes
## Prayer, Poetry, and Photography

Let me seek, then, the gift of silence, and poverty, and solitude,
where everything I touch is turned into prayer.
—Thomas Merton, *Thoughts in Solitude*

Becoming awake. Identifying spots of time. Recognizing the holy in
the ordinary. These are all important attitudes for developing one's
consciousness. Yet my query from chapter 2 remains: if one is awake,
can one become more awake? Readers of Merton's journals will, I sus-
pect, answer with an emphatic "yes" because we discover Merton not
just dallying in and with nature, but allowing the outside world, that
is, the landscape and its inhabitants, to become integral to his prayer.
Such integration represents a shift from intellectual knowing to more
pervasive experiential knowing. Merton is aware of the value of this
kind of knowing, even offering in a 1958 journal entry an anecdote
that illustrates his desire for this more intense kind of awareness. Merton recounts how, when reading in the toolshed (St. Anne's), a Carolina wren hopped onto his shoulder, then the page of his book, and,
after taking a look at him, flew away. Merton's reflection is revealing.

Man can know all about God's creation by examining its phenom-
ena, by dissecting and experimenting and this is all good. But it is
misleading, because with this kind of knowledge you *do not really*
know the beings you know. You only know *about* them. . . . You take
the thing not as it is, but as you want to investigate it. Your inves-

93

*why I could no longer direct experience*

tigation is valid, but artificial. There is something you cannot know about a wren by cutting it up in a laboratory and which you can only know if it remains fully and completely a wren, itself, and hops on your shoulder if it feels like it. . . . I want not only to observe but to *know* living things, and this implies a dimension of primordial famil-iarity which is simple and primitive and religious and poor. This is the reality I need, the vestige of God in His creatures. And the Light of God in my own soul. (SS 190; Merton's emphasis)

This kind of transformation of knowing enables Merton to articu-late his insights about contemplation and what he calls the True Self. Whereas his journals record the ministeps of this spiritual journey, Merton's published works on prayer offer convincing evidence of the significant effect of this ongoing transformation. For example, his ini-tial considerations of prayer in *Seeds of Contemplation* (1949) evolve into an enriched, more reflective version in the revised *New Seeds of Contemplation* (1962).

As Donald Grayston has effectively demonstrated, Merton's expe-rience during the dozen or so years between the publication of *Seeds of Contemplation* and *New Seeds of Contemplation*—a time of being more deeply influenced by the maternal and gratifying aspects of nature— enabled him to "remint" his concept of contemplation.[1] Whereas *Seeds* represents a traditional and orthodox approach to individual Catholic piety, *New Seeds* reveals Merton's spiritual and intellectual pilgrimage: it showcases a Merton "passing from a conventional member of a con-servative order in a conservative church to that of 'universal man,' to use a Sufi term."[2] The early dominant scholasticism (and dualism) of *Seeds*, notes Grayston, is balanced in *New Seeds* by a healthy dose of Zen and holistic thinking; reason is balanced by intuition, analysis by synthesis. Merton's experiential knowing allows him to realize that the "seed" of contemplation God sows in our souls helps us discover our essential unity with one another, yet "it is not we who choose to awaken ourselves, but God Who chooses to awaken us" (NSC 10). It is important to note that Merton's core understandings of prayer ar-ticulated in *Seeds* remain in the revised *New Seeds*; for example: "Every moment and every event of every man's life on earth plants something in his soul" (SC 17; NSC 14); "It is God's love that speaks to me in the birds and the stream" (SC 18; NSC 16); "A tree gives glory to God first of all by being a tree" (SC 24; NSC 29); individual forms of creation "constitute their holiness. . . . Their inscape is their sanctity" (SC 25; NSC 30). Nevertheless, some of the innovative sections in *New Seeds* unmistakably illustrate Merton's shift from intellectual knowing to experiential knowing.

One noticeable addition to *New Seeds* is the opening two chapters, which examine what contemplation is and what it is not. Merton is speaking not from textbook knowledge, but from the wealth and depth of his own experience of increased times of prayer in the silence of the woods. Thus, he is aptly able to testify that contemplation is *not* a function of the external self; contemplation has no relationship to the dualism of Descartes, is not an "affair of a passive and quiet temperament," not mere "prayerfulness, or a tendency to find peace and satisfaction in liturgical rites," not a trance, prophecy, or escape from conflict, or a sense of knowing what God is (NSC 7–13). Rather, as Merton asserts in the opening paragraph of chapter 1, "Contemplation is the highest expression of man's intellectual and spiritual life. It is that life itself, fully awake, fully active, fully aware that it is alive. It is spiritual wonder. It is spontaneous awe at the sacredness of life, of being . . . a sudden gift of awareness, an awakening to the Real within all that is real" (NSC 1, 3).

This deepened vision of contemplation—after more than a decade of increased solitude and commitment to the practice of contemplation—stresses the importance of becoming awake. *New Seeds* reads as if Merton were praying with pen in hand, intensifying and expanding over time the inclination that was already present. In *Seeds* he offers valuable insight into the practice of prayer and the virtues that lead to purity of heart; in *New Seeds* he expands on these insights with personal testimony. Merton just gets better! The final chapter of *New Seeds* dexterously displays Merton's ability to see creation differently—to imagine the whole world as a beloved garden in which God, the gardener of paradise, takes delight. This rhapsodic chapter, "The General Dance," presents an incarnational vision of God's love spilling over into creation, a love so powerful and intense that God could not bear to be only "distant, remote, transcendent and all powerful." God was *compelled* to "enter into His creation, emptying Himself, hiding Himself, as if He were not God but a creature" (NSC 292). The incarnate Christ, human and divine, is the very means of our unity, and everything—humans and all creation—is caught up in the ecstasy of the general dance. Our challenge, chides Merton, is to "become *aware* of His presence, consecrated by it, and transfigured in its light" (NSC 295; Merton's emphasis). Our challenge is to learn how to "play" in God's garden, to "let go of our own obsession with what we think is the meaning of it all . . . and follow Him in His mysterious, cosmic dance." Donald Grayston, using Merton's metaphors for prayer, summarizes the contrast between *Seeds* and *New Seeds* as the difference between looking inward at a well-ordered "citadel" and looking outward across a "wide, impregnable country." In praise of Merton's increased awareness and enlarging vision, Grayston comments, "He did this without moving from his metaphysical center, but by simply turning where he was, so to speak, 180 degrees."[3]

Merton's final paragraph of *New Seeds* reminds us that such an intensification of becoming aware, of seeing differently, is not difficult. Moments in nature call us to this new vision: "the starlit night," "migrating birds in autumn," "children" really being children, "love in our own hearts," "an old frog" landing "in a quiet pond with a solitary splash." These are the times we experience a new awakening and a "glimpse of the cosmic dance" (NSC 296–97).

Here, too, the quintessence of the Incarnation is evident: God has plunged into matter and in a particular and unique way into humanity in the person of Jesus. An incarnational theology recognizes the holiness of all creatures and the spark of divinity in all matter. It celebrates the "invasion" of matter by God, and the invitation to respond to the Divine. Merton recognizes the need for response. As he writes in *New Seeds*: "Contemplation is also the response to a call: a call from Him Who has no voice, and yet Who speaks in everything that is, and Who, most of all, speaks in the depths of our own being" (NSC 3). When Merton entitles a chapter in both *Seeds* and *New Seeds* "Everything

That Is, Is Holy" and notes in the preceding chapter that "it is God's love that warms me in the sun and God's love that sends the cold rain . . . that sends the winter days when I am cold and sick, and the hot summer when I labor and my clothes are full of sweat: but it is God Who breathes on me with light winds off the river and in the breezes out of the wood" (SC 18; NSC 16), he is identifying and acknowledging this spilling-over, creative intimacy of God. A. M. (Donald) Allchin, an Anglican scholar of orthodoxy and friend of Merton's, underscores Merton's deepening incarnational view, noting that his lectures to the novices in the 1960s focus on two points: incarnation and deification. In Allchin's words, what is essential is the recognition of "God coming to be with us where we are that we may come to be with him where he is; coming out of himself to us and our going out of ourselves to him."[4]

Though *Seeds* and *New Seeds* offer crisp evidence of Merton's enlarging vision, his journals record the often slow day-to-day action of grace and trace his persistent steps toward deeper experience of the Holy. At times, his glance is *outward:* his poetic eye captures the lyrical moment in a succinct phrase or an engaging metaphor; his astute observation of the weather subtly deepens his sense of and commitment to place; and his rhapsodic praise of nature often spontaneously overflows into praise of God. At other times his glance is *inward:* deep in prayer, Merton contemplates God's movement in his life, ruminates about the significance of his reading to his monastic practice, and assesses his growing relationship with God. Then, effortlessly, his meditation evolves into a celebration of the landscape around him. At still other times *inner and outer* geographies merge—not just in Merton's spiritual experience, but also in his apprehension and articulation of the experience. In such instances, Merton's attention to nature does not so much evoke a sequenced, reflective, inward glance at the holiness of the moment as it reveals the hidden wholeness and unity at the point of utter poverty (*le point vierge*) he experiences in the depth of his being.

This blending of inner and outer geography is not a thing, not an event, but a developing vision that suggests Merton is becoming ever more awake. To be sure, Merton's references to poetic imagery, metaphor, and weather continue throughout his journals, but the reader of multiple volumes of journal reflections—perhaps without consciously realizing it—discovers that Merton's developing intimacy with nature reveals an ongoing, sustaining transformation in consciousness and spirituality. Sociologists identify "parents, religious experience, and closeness to nature" as the primary influences that create a religious sensibility or point of view.[5] His parents having died while he was young, Merton is forced to rely on his monastic *horarium*, with its scheduled times for spiritual reading and contemplation, and his intimacy with nature to challenge, nourish, and enlarge his spiritual vision. Indeed, such a journeying deeper into God through the medium of nature creates a spiritual substratum that prepares Merton for his radical and pointed response to Rachel Carson. Using contemporary parlance, one could suggest that this transformative process represents the gradual "greening" of Merton's spirituality. It is worth examining some of these journal entries to witness the transformative process in action and discover how overwhelmingly influential nature is in Merton's spirituality and, indeed, in his full human development.

## Nature Overflowing into Prayer

On the feast of Saint Bernard (August 20) in 1947, for example, Merton comments on the limitations of his evening meditation, then continues: "After Night Office I stood in the door by the kitchen and looked at the stars and the sky paling out behind Rohan's knob, and the barns and the water tower. How fierce and efficient that tank makes this place look—geared for battle. My God, lock me in Your will, imprison me in Your Love and Your Wisdom, and draw me to Yourself. I will belong to You. I will not be afraid of anything for I shall remain in Your hands and never leave You" (ES 101). In this passage Merton offers precise details of the evening landscape, then slips easily into an earnest and somewhat formal prayer imploring God to use every means available to bring about union of monk with the Divine. In return, Merton abandons himself totally to being possessed by that Divinity. What begins as a bit of verbal wandering, of enumerating the points of nature in the twilight landscape, becomes grist for his fierce desire to be completely possessed by God.

This same movement from articulating aspects of nature to recognizing and praising God can be detected in numerous journal passages. At times the movement is subtle and evocative; at other times it is more transparent and exuberant. Notice the subtle slip into meditative reflection in this short passage: "The sun is rising. All the green trees are full of birds, and their song comes up out of the wet bowers of the orchard. Crows swear pleasantly in the distance, and in the depths of my soul sits God" (SJ 188).

In other, longer entries Merton is more transparent about his realization that nature moves him to deeper prayer. He begins: "A lovely cool, dazzling bright afternoon yesterday. Blue sky, clouds, silence, and the immense sunlit sweep of St. Malachy's field." After this initial catalogue of the elements, he comments at length on the vegetation, "blooming with delicate, heather-like purple blossoms and bees were busy in them," then shifts into a recognition of the "continuity of grace in my life" with this comment: "An entirely beautiful, transfigured moment of love for God and the need for complete confidence in Him in everything, without reserve, even when almost nothing can be understood" (DWL 9).

Not only flowers and blue sky attract Merton's prayerful awareness. Even in the dead of a Kentucky winter, nature claims his attention and feeds his prayer. Consider, for example, his January 1, 1964, entry: "Cold grey afternoon, much snow, woods bright with snow loom out of the dark, totally new vision of the Vineyard Knob. Dark, etched out with snow, standing in obscurity and in a kind of spaciousness I had never seen before. The wide sweep of snow on St. Benedict's field. I furiously climbed the Lake Knob, wonderful woods! Slid down, tore my pants on barbed wire, came back through the vast fields of snow. Sense of God all day." This shift to the focus on God spurs Merton to write several paragraphs about his current reading project: Rudolf Bultmann's idea of belief as a moment-to-moment challenge. He concludes this section of his journal entry with a Bultmann quotation he intends to be his prayerful mantra "at the head of a New Year, not of

the dragon but of the Lord: 'If in Christian belief in God we understand the claims of the "moment" to be those of the "thou" and of the
demand to love, then it is clear that this crisis is in the constant struggle
of hate against love and that this crisis becomes acute in every encounter with the "thou" which thoughtlessly or selfishly we would disregard, maintaining our own rights and our own interests, in contempt
or in undisguised hate' " (DWL 52–53). As a New Year's resolution, a
commitment to identify and respond to the challenge to love at every
moment is indeed an appropriate guiding prayer.

This same impulse to regard nature as prelude to prayer continues
throughout Merton's journals, yet it takes on a note of new intensity after he gains permission to spend more time in the cinderblock
hermitage he names Saint Mary of Mount Carmel. In April 1961 he
writes: "The evening sky over the valley. Long lines of clouds travelling
in strong cold wind toward the east. *Janua Coeli* [Gate of Heaven].
How different prayer is here. Clarity—direction—to Christ the Lord
for the great gift—the passage out of this world to the Father, entry
into the kingdom. I know what I am here for. May I be faithful to
this awareness. *'Le project* [sic] *initial?'* ['The initial project?']" (TTW
108–9). Although Merton does not identify *"le project initial,"* it is
probably safe to surmise he is thinking of his call to live full-time as a
hermit in this simple structure not quite a mile from the monastery.

## Prayer Evolving into Praise of the Natural World

The reverse movement is also evident in Merton's journal. Sometimes
a period of inner reflection, spiritual reading, or sustained contemplation erupts, not in distraction by nature, but in celebration and praise
of it. For example, barely two months after Merton has been given permission to pray outside the cloistered area of the monastery grounds,
he records in his journal the fruits of a day of recollection spent mull-
ing over the book of Ecclesiasticus, even setting down in six points his
spiritual insights. But after writing at considerable length about "the
secret and inexpressible seed of contemplation planted in the depths of
our soul and awakening it with an immediate and inexpressible contact

Saint Mary of Mount Carmel: Merton's hermitage. (Photo by Thomas Merton)

with the Living Word," Merton shifts into a reflection on the power of scripture for him and by extension the power of nature: "By the reading of Scripture I am so renewed that all nature seems renewed round me and with me. The sky seems to be more pure, a cooler blue, the trees a deeper green, light is sharper on the outlines of the forest and the hills and the whole world is charged with the glory of God and I feel fire and music in the earth under my feet" (ES 348–50). Most of us recognize the profound influence scripture can have on our lives when we really allow the words to sink deeply into our hearts; but notice how, for Merton, all of nature is also transformed: more intense colors, sharper outlines, and an exuberant echo of Gerard Manley Hopkins's famous lines: "The world is charged with the grandeur of God / It will flame out like shining from shook foil."[6]

With a note of humor, this same movement from prayer to praise of nature occurs during the Christmas season of 1952. Merton is not only meditating on the liturgical texts but also rehearsing his duties as deacon for High Mass. He practices singing the ancient chants pacing back and forth in the woods and notes in his journal: "So this week I sing the Epiphany Gospel, and, as I sing it, the trees of the woods come before me. . . . The questions of the Magi and the plot of Herod. *Ubi est qui natus est rex Judaeorum?* [Where is he that is born King of the Jews? (Matthew 2:2)] I know where He is. He and I live in the trees" (ES 464). With a wry comment, Merton is moving beyond simple meditation on scripture and the mystery of the Incarnation to savor the unity he experiences with God in the woods. In the words of the theologian Sallie McFague, Merton is discovering that "the world is our meeting place with God . . . as the body of God, it is wondrously, awesomely, divinely mysterious."[7]

Later that same year (1952) Merton is reflecting on the Old Testament figure of Noah and the symbolism of the rainbow. In Merton's view, Noah's simplicity allows him to understand the "alliance between man and God" and nature as "signs and pledges of our union with God." But here Merton pivots from nature as religious symbol to the particularity of the landscape before him: "Now the rising sun comes over the bank of lowly slate-colored clouds out there, and I can no longer look straight into the East, beyond the woods where the crows are breaking silence." With a comment about the nearby scarecrows, caught and dazzling in the fiery rays of our sun-star, he itemizes other inhabitants of the scene: "The door of the hayloft in the cowbarn yawns into the rising sun, the grass is full of crickets, and black birds whistle softly under the water tower" (SS 9).

A few days later, as he contemplates the value of St. Anne's, the toolshed where he enjoys more solitude and extended prayer, he writes:

I am now almost completely convinced that I am only really a monk when I am alone in the old toolshed Reverend Father gave me. . . .

True, I have the will of a monk in the community. But I have the *prayer* of a monk in the silence of the woods and the toolshed. To begin with: the place is simple, and really poor with the bare poverty I need worse than any other medicine and which I never seem to get. And silent. And inactive—materially. Therefore the Spirit is busy here. What is easier than to discuss mutually with You, O God, the three crows that flew by in the sun with light flashing on their rubber wings? Or the sunlight coming quietly through the cracks in the boards? Or the crickets in the grass? You are sanctified in them when, beyond the blue hills, my mind is lost in Your intentions for us all who live with hope under the servitude of corruption! (SS 14)

Notice that the inward glance at his spiritual state shifts to an outward glance that recognizes and embraces the particular features of nature that are currently part of his environment and therefore part of his prayer. What begins as attention to God's transcendence transforms into recognition of God's immanence. A similar reflection strikes Merton a few years later when he enjoys the opportunity to spend long periods of time and occasional overnights at the hermitage, Saint Mary of Mount Carmel:

Everything about this hermitage simply fills me with joy . . . it is the place God has given me after so much prayer and longing—but without my deserving it—and it is a delight. I can imagine no other joy on earth than to have such a place and to be at peace in, to live in silence, to think and write, to listen to the wind and to all the voices of the wood, to live in the shadow of the big cedar cross, to prepare for my death and my exodus to the heavenly country, to love my brothers and all people, and to pray for the whole world and for peace and good sense among men. So it is "my place" in the scheme of things, and that is sufficient! (DWL 209)

Here Merton's prayer of gratitude for the totality of the experience of solitude moves into delineating the natural and human elements of his life and a recognition that at last he is a round peg in a round hole. He fits. The desires of his inner being are being influenced and nourished by his solitude in the woods.

103

Merton is not the only writer who tries to articulate the immanent spark of divinity that solitude in nature reveals. The nature writer Annie Dillard, for example, in her award-winning book *Pilgrim at Tinker Creek,* remarks that divine power is not something that travels, that can be "there" but not "here." Rather, as Dillard phrases it, divinity "rolls along the mountain ridges like a fireball, shooting off a spray of sparks at random, and will not be trapped, slowed, grasped, fetched, peeled, or aimed." The divine spark is always around us and in us; our challenge is to "catch it if you can."[8] Supported by his reading of Meister Eckhart's description of the divine spark and open to the energy of God at work in all of creation, Merton is often involved in a game of catch. His ability to play that game—that is, to join in the general dance of creation—allows him to move back and forth between the specifics of nature and the movements of grace in the depths of his being. Indeed, drawing from the practice of *theoria physica* promoted by the Greek Fathers, who realized that God can be recognized in created things, Merton is well equipped—naturally and theologically—to celebrate God in creation. As the environmental ethicist Dennis Patrick O'Hara argues, Merton discovers how creation "can inform our thoughts and prayers, acting as cables, medium, and message."[9] In his Working Notebook 15, containing, among other jottings, notes for poems and ideas for his quixotic yet linguistically and spiritually rich anti-poem, *Cables to the Ace,* Merton reveals how prayer moves into the arena of nature and invites a refreshing experience of unity:

> My worship is a blue sky and ten thousand
> crickets in the deep wet grass of the field.
> My vow is the silence under their
> Sound. I support the woodpecker and the dove.
> Together we learn the norms. The plowed and planted field
> says: it is my turn. And several of us
> begin to sing.[10]

Here Merton not only celebrates the splendor of nature and his intent to interact responsibly with it—symbolized by his commitment to the woodpecker and the dove—but also admits how his worship and nature's praise of God are intertwined. The field initiates a moment of celebration, yet the use of "my" is unclear. Does the field claim it is *its* turn, or does the field indicate it is *my* turn, meaning the speaker, Merton? Regardless, "several of us begin to sing": together, sky, crickets, birds, field, and Merton experience a moment of noisy celebratory worship.

## Merging Inner and Outer Landscapes

In these special and increasingly frequent moments when Merton's inner and outer worlds merge, when the distinction between external and internal geography dissolves, his writing reveals not a sequential or linear movement between prayer and noticing his surroundings, but an integrated experience of life as unity. His Lenten reflection for February 27, 1950, for example, illustrates this new vision.

> The first Sunday of Lent, as I now know, is a great feast. Christ has sanctified the desert and in the desert I discovered it. The woods have all become young in the discipline of spring, but it is the discipline of expectancy only. Which one cut more keenly? The February sunlight, or the air? There are no buds. Buds are not guessed or even thought of this early in Lent. But the wilderness shines with promise. The land is first in simplicity and strength. Everything foretells the coming of the holy spring. I had never before spoken freely or so intimately with woods, hills, buds, water and sky. On this great day, however, they understood their position and they remained mute in the presence of the Beloved. Only His light was obvious and eloquent. My brother and sister, the light and the water. The stump and the stone. The tables of rock. The blue, naked sky. Tractor tracks, a little waterfall. And Mediterranean solitude. I thought of Italy after my Beloved had spoken and was gone. (ES 412)

In this passage Merton begins with an acknowledgment of Lent and its desert symbolism, but he moves to the concurrent season of spring and the promise of new life. His Franciscan embrace of the elements of nature as his brother and sister, and the twice-mentioned Beloved, indicates that there is, for Merton, no separation between inner and outer worlds, no distinction between the Jesus-Resurrection and the spring-resurgence, no distinction between the material and the spiritual. This merging, this confluence of inner and outer landscapes, becomes for Merton an experience of hidden wholeness. As he writes in *The Inner Experience* about the importance of the Incarnation and the power of landscape to explode, like a clap of thunder, into spiritual insight and transformation: "The important thing in contemplation is not gratification and rest, but awareness, life, creativity, and freedom . . . it is a flash of the lightning of divinity piercing the darkness of nothingness and sin" (IE 10, 34, 37–38).

Multiple examples in the journals reveal Merton's increasing awareness of the complementary harmony of his inner and outer worlds. For example, early in his monastic life he writes: "All the hills and woods are red and brown and copper, and the sky is clear with one or two very small clouds. And a buzzard comes by and investigates me, but I am not dead yet. This landscape is getting so saturated with my prayers and psalms and the books I read that it is becoming incomparably rich for me" (ES 124). In his published version of this passage, Merton edits his original perception with some additional telling phrases. He reads his books "under the trees, looking over the wall, not at the world but at our forest, our solitude" (SJ 69). The inclusive pronoun "our" is significant: Merton is not slipping into the monastic plural to indicate the shared ownership of goods demanded by his vow of poverty, but identifying a lived reality of oneness: both Merton and the forest are in an intense, quiet mode, a shared solitude interlaced with *lectio divina* as well as psalms of praise. The convergence of that wonderful saturation of the woods with prayer and Merton's being with nature is not a onetime occurrence. The experience is again beautifully expressed in a July 9, 1961, journal entry:

> Dawn at the hermitage. I slept until 3 and came up here to say the office—the long way round by the road. Very thin end of a moon in the morning sky. Crows bothering an owl. Once again—the office is entirely different in its proper (natural) setting, out from under the fluorescent lights. There Lauds is torpor and vacuum. Here it is in

harmony with all the singing birds under the bright sky. Everything you have on your lips in praising God is there before you—hills, dew, light, birds, growing things. . . . Nothing in the liturgy of light is lost. I saw in the middle of the Benedicite the great presence of the sun that had just risen behind the cedars (same time and place as Trinity Sunday). And now under the pines the sun has made a great golden basilica of fire and water. (TTW 140)

What an awesome experience: the liturgy of light. In comparison with a more formal and perhaps stodgy celebration of this early monastic Hour usually chanted at daybreak, Merton experiences a unique blending of inner and outer reality, his voice joining all creation in praise. His spiritual insight is akin to the counsel of Raimundo Panikkar, a philosopher, scientist, and theologian who urges us to discover our own "monkhood," that is, the contemplative dimension innate in every human being. Paradoxically, however, cautions Panikkar, once this monkhood becomes ritualized, it runs the risk of substituting the means for the end—a pathway that leads to a kind of religious totalitarianism.[11] This observation probably would have resonated with Merton (IE 78).

Although Merton originally went to the monastery to find his place in the world, to acquire a monastic perspective and then practice living out of it (as he writes on March 3, 1951), he becomes increasingly aware of how important it is to be fully human, that is, fully cognizant of being *humus*—earth, part of the very stuff of creation. Several of Panikkar's sutras, or aphoristic principles, reflect this same fundamental challenge: the primacy of being over doing; the priority of silence over word; the primacy of the sacred ("the sacredness of the secular"), and the unity of Mother Earth preceding the brotherhood of man.[12] The ideal for each of us is to discover, as Merton does when praying in nature, one essential truth: "The monk lives in communion with the cosmos; he is in touch with the sap that runs through the Earth—and with good and evil spirits alike."[13] Nevertheless, this spiritual insight, awesome as it is, is not unique to Panikkar, Merton, or vowed religious. As the MacArthur honoree and ecofeminist Susan Griffin has phrased it: "We know ourselves to be made from this earth. We know this earth is made from our bodies. For we see ourselves. And we are nature. We are nature seeing nature. We are nature with a concept of nature. Nature weeping. Nature speaking of nature to nature."[14]

Many snippets of journal entries reinforce the premise of Merton's growth toward this new vision. During his first overnight in the hermitage, for example, with its intensity of silence as he is reciting Compline before an icon of Mary, Merton notes that "this was the way things are supposed to be." In the morning when he recites Lauds, he feels "very much alive, and real, and awake, surrounded by silence and penetrated by truth. Wonderful smell of pre-dawn woods and fields in the cold night!" (DWL 154). A few months before he moves to the hermitage permanently, in 1965, he writes: "Peace and beauty of Easter morning sunrise: deep green grass, soft winds, the woods turning green on the hills across the valley (and here too). I got up and said the old office of Lauds, and there was a wood thrush singing fourth-tone mysteries in the deep ringing pine wood (the 'unconscious' wood) behind the hermitage" (DWL 231). Such an experience also calls to mind the early twentieth-century advice of John Burroughs. With pointed allusion to 1 Corinthians 13:13, Burroughs identifies "three precious resources: books, friends, and nature, and the greatest of these, at least the most constant and always at hand, is nature."[15]

Merging of inner and outer landscapes appears also in a more deliberately crafted "public" prayer recorded in Merton's journal for May 21, 1961, and in *Conjectures of a Guilty Bystander* as a "Prayer to God My Father on the Vigil of Pentecost" (TTW 120; CGB 177–78). In this compelling experience of oneness, Merton begins by citing the blue sky, the flycatcher, the flowers of the tulip tree, the sweet air, and a host of other creatures who praise God by being who they are; "you have placed me here this morning in the midst of them. And here I am." Merton shifts then to his own doubts and confusion and the great invitation to become God's friend. "Here I will learn from the words of Your Friends to be Your Friend. . . . If I have any choice to make, it is to live and even die here." The final lines of Merton's prayer are an invocation to the Father to teach him to be a man of peace with the "courage to suffer for truth" (TTW 120–21). A year earlier, on

the feast of Pentecost—a special celebration of the Spirit present everywhere in the universe—Merton realizes that saying Lauds outdoors
in the woods "against the background of waking birds and sunrise"
gives him an experience of the *"full meaning"* of this prayer of praise.
At the occasional *Om* of the bullfrog or the cry of the whippoorwill,
he experiences *le point vierge* of the day when all creation asks God if
it is time to be. At this dramatic moment of breaking day, Merton is
one with the universe. Being awake to such moments when inner and
outer worlds merge deepens Merton's spirituality, but it also precipi-
tates spots of time (discussed in chapter 3) that create bodily shivers.

In becoming awake and developing a habit of listening—what
Saint Benedict called "opening the ear of your heart"—Merton comes
to understand that immersion or saturation in solitude and contemplation is essential for discovering his identity. One could say his relationship with nature is not casual, but causal and paradoxical; indeed, as
he notes in a June 4, 1963, entry, he both finds and loses himself in
solitude, acknowledging this "cocoon" stage in his ongoing transformation (DWL 327–28). Meditating in a field accompanied by fire-
flies is not, as one disgruntled critic charged, "narcissistic regression,"
but rather, as Merton replies, a "complete awakening of identity and
rapport! It implies an awareness and acceptance of one's place in the
whole, first the whole of creation, then the whole plan of Redemption"
(DWL 250). Four years later, writing to Dom Francis Decroix, Merton
is more precise about the value of saturating oneself in solitude: "The
contemplative has nothing to tell you except to reassure you and say
that if you dare to penetrate your own silence and risk the sharing of
that solitude with the lonely other who seeks God through you, then
you will truly recover the light and the capacity to understand what is
beyond words and beyond explanations because it is too close to be
explained: it is the intimate union in the depths of your own heart, of
God's spirit and your own secret inmost self, so that you and He are in
all truth One Spirit."[16]

Paradoxically, the increased solitude of the hermitage enables Merton to realize that finding himself in God means also finding others
in God. Attention to nature awakens deeper insights and broader vi-

sion. Merton crafts this understanding for the published version of his journal: solitude in the hermitage is making him see that "the universe is my home and I am nothing if not part of it. . . . Only as part of the world's fabric and dynamism can I find my true being in God. . . . This, I discover here in the hermitage, not mentally only but in depth and wholeness, especially, for instance, in the ability to sleep. At the monastery, frogs kept me awake. There are frogs here but they do not keep me awake. They are a comfort, an extension of my own being" (VC 156).

## Poetry—An Extension of Prayer

When we acknowledge how insistent Merton is on the importance of becoming awake so that vision is both widened and deepened, we can begin to appreciate how his poetry—especially those poems published in the early 1960s—always moves beyond cursory lyrical imagery and traditional religious devotion to embody his experience of prayer. In "Song for Nobody," for example, a single yellow flower becomes a

> gentle sun
> In whose dark eye
> Someone is awake . . .
> O, wide awake! (CP 337)

The urgency of being awake sprinkled periodically through the journal entries resounds in this poem like a trumpet call: do not miss this advice, heed this invitation!

Similarly, the bobwhite in "O Sweet Irrational Worship" represents both call and intimate response. The poem's persona claims he is "light, / Bird and wind." His "leaves sing"; he is a "lake of blue air"; he is "earth, earth" out of which "rises the bobwhite" ready to offer "his foolish worship" (CP 345). Why this bird as symbol for union and communion with God? As early as December 1958, while waiting in the town library for his ride back to the monastery, Merton browsed through a bird book, and then enumerated the various species in his journal, commenting that the bobwhite is his totem bird (SS 238). We know that Merton had access to field glasses and enjoyed identifying pairs of birds that nested near the hermitage. Avid birders may want to suggest one reason Merton considers the bobwhite his totem, or "familiar": the song of the bobwhite is shared by monogamous pairs. According to some ornithologists, the male of the species usually begins the introductory notes of the melody, which is then completed by the female. How fitting an image for Merton, the contemplative, intent on sustaining and deepening his bonds of intimacy with God. Once the poem's persona realizes he is "earth, earth," it is easy to assume the guise of the bobwhite yearning for his mate, his fulfillment:

> Out of my grass heart
> Rises the bobwhite.
> Out of my nameless weeds
> His foolish worship.

Those intent on developing a spiritual life can only surmise—and through grace, experience—how powerful this kind of "wasting time with God" is, and how such productive foolishness initiates a response from the Beloved. Whereas Merton's frequent journal entries allude to many sustained moments of silent communion, this poem not only validates but lyrically proclaims the power of the experience.

In "Night-Flowering Cactus," another poem written during the 1960s, Merton presents us with an image of the rarely seen "sudden Eucharist" of the cactus blossom that transforms viewers who will "live forever in its echo: / You will never be the same again" (CP 351–52). The transfigured Merton understands well the particular grace offered in ordinary moments to those who are aware; his poem about a singular and mysterious event captures a sense of the unpredictable outpouring of God and invites us into that same vulnerability. Yet if that one awesome nocturnal experience is not offered, Merton insists that silent, hidden growing is nevertheless taking place. In "Love Winter When the Plant Says Nothing," the apparent "daily zero" of perceived change is in reality the seedbed of inner fire, an "unsetting sun" that grows in secret (CP 353). Merton's gift for seeing beyond the surface—his

commitment to becoming awake, to responding to significant transformative moments, and to finding God in the ordinary—continues
to reveal and support his deepening spirituality. Coming from the pen
of a writer more than forty years ago, these images continue to affect
the reader and witness the power of mystical language fashioned in the
fiery forge of contemplation. These images continue to urge the reader
toward an encounter with nature, believing that "all that is, is holy."

Although we don't regard Merton primarily as a storyteller, his
journals and poems represent an unfolding personal story full of paradox, irony, and contradiction that in the end reveal spiritual integration and healing. Like Rilke, one of his favorite poets, Merton sees
the value of letting the things of the Earth become his familiars so
that the important work of transformation—of yoking Earth and consciousness—can create a new unity.[17] This work of yoking Earth and
consciousness can perhaps best be illustrated by a brief inspection of
two published prose poems, "Fire Watch, July 4, 1952" and "Hagia
Sophia." The first, originally in volume 2 of Merton's journals, becomes the more highly crafted epilogue for *The Sign of Jonas* (1953), a
"kind of story" that reveals Merton's emotional and spiritual response
to his contemplative life and offers an archetype of the Jonas-like life of
a monk.[18] The second, a 1959 response to Victor Hammer's painting
of Mary placing a crown on the head of the Child Jesus in her arms,
was published first in a limited, handset edition, and in 1963 as the
concluding poem in *Emblems of a Season of Fury* (CP 363–71). The ten
years between the revised publication of these two works sharply illustrate—as did the transformation from *Seeds* to *New Seeds*—a deepening
communion with the Divine in nature that is becoming more frequent
and more pervasive in Merton's prayer. One could say that prayer so
thoroughly engages Merton that it becomes both background and
foreground for these published writings.

## "Fire Watch, July 4, 1952" and "Hagia Sophia"

"Fire Watch" employs the classical journey motif of going down fa-
vored by Virgil and Dante, as well as the Christian motif of spiritual

ascent, such as the ladder of John Climacus and Mount Carmel of John of the Cross. Merton's text reveals not only his knowledge of these literary antecedents but also his emotional and spiritual response to his own unique monastic journey. One must go down in order to go up. As Donald St. John has cogently noted, this prose poem of the "watcher" who sees into the heart of reality is a "tribute to [Merton's] own deepening experience of its geography"; it is significant primarily because of Merton's "eye for detail, his love of nature, and his ability to evoke a sense of place."[19] In his role as night watchman, Merton focuses on both time and place, clocking in at appointed stations to confirm there are no sparks or flames that could quickly consume the wooden monastery. But with his expanding vision, he interweaves his travels through the darkened monastery terrain with a prayerful apostrophe to God and a deepening sense of the ancient holy story of the place, ultimately as his biographer Michael Mott notes, offering "praise for, and loyalty to, a place"[20]—now *his* place.

Engaging in a process of excavating the history of Gethsemani as well as his own monastic history, which is still full of questions, Merton walks through the monastery. His walks also function as an examination of conscience, an invitation to let go of the past and—as Rilke advised the young poet—to live with the questions. Merton offers us vivid word pictures with synchronic details of dishes and silverware for postulants who eat in the congested hallways, and desks for the scholastics in the similarly crowded library, as well as diachronic events of the "geological strata" of the lower level of the south wing of the monastery, which reaches up to the tower itself. His geography is both horizontal and vertical, contemporary and historical. In Merton's consciousness, stairwells murmur the events of his personal past and walls whisper stories of years gone by. Having descended into the belly of the monastery, he finds it is time to climb "the trembling, twisted stair into the belfry." It is time to go up. Opening the door, Merton walks out "upon a vast sea of darkness and of prayer" (SJ 350–60).

Exposed to the night wind and the dark world of nature that curiously reminds him of death, Merton sees the "whole valley flooded with moonlight. . . . Now the huge chorus of living beings rises up out of the world beneath my feet: life singing in the watercourses, throbbing in the creeks and the fields and the trees, choirs of millions and millions of jumping and flying and creeping things. And far above me the cool sky opens upon the frozen distance of the stars." Merton is at the peak of his journey, physically and spiritually. Overcome with awe at the power of creation and the presence of the Word-made-flesh within, Merton experiences the immanence of Reality Itself. Asking God if he sees and remembers various places on the monastery ground, Merton has to admit that for God, time and place dissolve: "There is no leaf that is not in Your care . . . no water in the shales that was not hidden there by Your wisdom." Eternity is in the here and now. "With You there is no dialogue. . . . You are found in communion: Thou in me and I in Thee and Thou in them and they in me." In this epiphanic moment of integrated inner and outer geographies—of intense communion with all that is—the "Voice of God is heard in Paradise." What is the message? With a list of paradoxes that confirms the uniqueness of God's ways, Merton comes to understand that all is forgiven. Ultimately, God's great gift is "mercy within mercy within mercy." Characteristically, Merton ends this prose poem with one lyrical sentence celebrating the dawn—dewdrops "like sapphires in the grass" and leaves that "stir behind the hushed flight of an escaping dove." In essence, "Fire Watch" is a hymn to solitude and the necessity of being awake—not just to the potential of wood-destroying fire, but to the potential of the great, fiery Spirit of God that is "born in our own souls as quietly as the breath of our own being" (SJ 349–62).

Perhaps one of the reasons readers find "Fire Watch" so moving is that Merton is creating a paradox of his own: articulating the inarticulable, capturing the ineffable in a "story" with archetypal imagery that occurs not only at the apex of the monastery tower, but also in the depths of the heart at the juncture of inner and outer landscapes. Merton, the poet-mystic who understands biblical symbols as well as experiences of contemplative intuition, presents us with a narrative of both personal and universal significance.

His second well-known prose poem, "Hagia Sophia," can be

viewed as a companion piece to and a development of "Fire Watch" in that it, too, blends the natural and spiritual, inner and outer landscapes. "Hagia Sophia," also structured on time—both chronological and theological or mystical time—begins, one might say, where "Fire Watch" leaves off. The realization of mercy at the conclusion of the 1952 text is the starting point of this later meditation on Sophia—Wisdom—the feminine, creative aspect of God. As Sister Thérèse Lentfoehr has pointed out in her study of the theology and poetics of this work, "Hagia Sophia" integrates and celebrates "Oriental opposites basic to all beings: *animus* and *anima*, *eros* and *agape*, the One and the Many. The Divine Persons are at once Sophia and the feminine child 'playing before God, the Creator in His universe, playing before him at all times, playing in the world' (Proverbs 8)." Sophia is the "feminine, dark, yielding, tender part of the power, justice, creative dynamism of the Father"; Mary is a "personal manifestation of Sophia."[21]

Although this prose poem is divided into Dawn, Early Morning, High Morning, and Sunset, literary scaffolding used by Rilke and other modern poets, it is more about theological or mystical time than clock time, and it offers the reader not questions but the *fruit* of intense encounter with God. The poem's persona is already in paradise, awakening as one man, as Adam, and as all creation at *le point vierge* of the day, "confronting reality and finding it to be gentleness." The six repetitions of "gentle" and "gentleness" early in the text are synonyms for the great gift of mercy discovered and celebrated at the climax of "Fire Watch." Gentleness, or mercy, is always the touch of the One who desires us to "come out of the confused primordial dark night into consciousness." In section 3 of "Hagia Sophia" Merton says it more plainly: "Sophia is the mercy of God in us." This statement is not a part of a didactic lecture, but testimony to a felt experience of how mercy knots the broken string of relationships. Important to note also is that "Hagia Sophia" is permeated with nature imagery from its opening sentence: "There is in all visible things an invisible fecundity, a dimmed light, a meek namelessness, a hidden wholeness." Additional layers of nature imagery reinforce this mystical tone: "innocent visages of flowers," "the dewy earth." We discover that the "stars rejoice," the "sun burns," Sophia is the "Divine Life" in all creation, and Mary is the perfect reflection of Sophia, who ushers God into creation. Echoing Gerard Manley Hopkins's tribute to Mary, whose "hand leaves his light / Sifted to suit our sight," and celebrating the Christ who "plays in ten thousand places,"[22] Merton creates a stunning hymn to the unfolding creative love of God/Wisdom/Sophia/Mary. The text revolves not around questions, but around an assertion: "There is in all visible things an invisible fecundity, a dimmed light, a meek namelessness, a hidden wholeness." From the opening lines that affirm the divine spark within all creation holding it in being, to its concluding poignant picture of the incarnate Christ beginning to make his way through human history, Merton offers the reader vivid testimony of divine activity. The initial call to awaken from sleep comes full circle to an anticipated innocent and vulnerable sleep, as the focus of the poem moves to Christ, the "destitute wanderer . . . a homeless God, lost in the night, without papers," who (an allusion to Matthew 8:20) commits himself to lie down "under the sweet stars of the world and entrusts Himself to sleep" (CP 363–71).

One might be tempted to ask: so what? Now that we know that Merton's journal writings reveal various interactions with nature—celebration of the landscape evolving into meditation and formal prayer; contemplative reflection spilling over into exuberant praise of nature; and passages in which nature and prayer are so intertwined that they reveal a new harmony and unity—what is the significance of that knowledge? Granted, scholars have already probed Merton's public journals (*A Secular Journal, The Sign of Jonas, Conjectures of a Guilty Bystander,* and *A Vow of Conversation,* which he revised to some degree for publication), looking through biographical, theological, psychological, and thematic lenses as a way of determining Merton's preoccupations in these specific years. But now that we have access to all seven volumes of his journals, the information base shifts.

Tracing when and how nature influences Merton's spirituality through the pages of the complete journals offers us a unique window onto his maturing spiritual life and provides a richer context for reading published works such as "Fire Watch" and "Hagia Sophia." These texts do not represent a literary diversion or outlet for Merton, but reveal the very fabric of his thinking, living, praying. "Fire Watch" and "Hagia Sophia" capture and articulate epiphanic moments in Merton's life and simultaneously evoke epiphanies for us, his readers. They lyrically represent the core insights of Merton's ever-deepening spirituality, which we see spill over into every aspect of his life, including his ongoing writing of poetry and his late-found fascination with photography. Both activities, springing from his vocation as writer and his avocation as photographer, are not tangents or distractions in Merton's life; rather, in the light of his published journals, Merton's poetry and photography illustrate more richly the overflowing of his prayerful interaction with nature. Both art forms are compelling verbal and visual examples of how in his later years inner and outer landscapes twine, merge, and reveal an integrated spirituality. Both art forms contribute to our broader understanding and respect for this writer-monk who, in almost every instance, defies categorization.

## Photography—Visual Prayer

It should be no surprise that Merton eventually became fascinated with photography. In his early childhood he saw his father painting landscapes; in his late adolescent years he was enamored of the mosaics in the churches in Rome, and he later cherished the small icon of Elias on his hermitage wall; as a young adult he enjoyed figure drawing and critiquing baroque paintings; and during his monastery years the study of Eastern religious experience inspired him to explore calligraphies representing Chinese thought.[23] Photography allowed Merton another creative outlet through which to discover the beauty and spiritual meaning of the ordinary. Using at first a monastery camera and in early 1968 one that belonged to John Howard Griffin (the author, most famously, of *Black Like Me*), Merton began experimenting with photos of vistas looming beyond the toolshed windows, close-ups of tree stumps, ridges in wooden doors, arrangements of rocks, and striations in bark. Griffin had numerous occasions to observe Merton's attraction "to the movement of wheat in the wind, the textures of snow,

A tree root on the hermitage porch. (Photo by Thomas Merton)

paint-spattered cans, stone, crocuses blossoming through weeds—or again, the woods in all their hours, from the first fog of morning, through noonday stillness, to evening quiet."[24]

A few cameras and hundreds of photos later, Merton's commitment to contemplation, his fondness for praying out of doors, and his study of Zen converge to make these forays with a camera another prayer experience in nature. September 1964 seems to be a particularly productive time. His journal entries frequently mention being outdoors with his camera and even hint at a growing obsession with photography. On September 24, for example, Merton notes in his journal, "The whole place is full of fantastic and strange subjects—a mine of Zen photography" (DWL 147). Two days later, after his camera has been repaired in town, he exclaims: "Camera back. Love affair with camera. Darling camera, so glad to have you back!" (DWL 149). Merton's framing of scenes is testimony to his ability to see the integral beauty of natural and man-made objects—to see into the reality of nature, expand his awareness, and know at a deeper level how "their inscape is their sanctity" (NSC 30).

Griffin attests to Merton's ability to appreciate the integrity of each aspect of nature: "He did not seek to capture or possess, and certainly not to arrange the objects he photographed. He lent his vision and his lenses to them in a real way . . . but he allowed the objects to remain true to themselves and to reveal themselves, and he trusted that 'the connections would somehow be made.'"[25] Indeed, observes Griffin, "going out to the thing and giving oneself to it, allowing it to communicate its essence, allowing it to say what it will, reveal what it will . . . was one of Merton's profoundest orientations."[26] Before he left for his ill-fated trip to Asia, Griffin asserts, Merton's poetic eye had developed into a "photographer's eye."[27]

Nevertheless, photography, for Merton, is not about freeze-framing the external world; it is, the current Merton archivist, Paul Pearson, notes, more about pointing to the trailhead, inviting the viewer to a spiritual journey, raising questions, and creating opportunities to pause and reflect on "the meaning of the spiritual."[28] Photography becomes a Zen experience that "seeks not to *explain* but to *pay attention*, to *become aware*, to be *mindful*, in other words to develop a certain *kind of consciousness*" (ZBA 38; Merton's emphasis). Taking pictures in 1968 in California, Merton is intent on replicating in black and white the unity he experiences: "I wonder how the photos will turn out that I took of old logs with strange abstract patterns on them" (OSM 119). Such photos of trees, logs, rocks, and shoreline, comments the literary scholar Ross Labrie, represent "not only the beauty of the sea rocks but also the 'interior landscape' of himself in the implicitly collaborative photograph produced by both himself and nature."[29] Merton's advice to the Trappist community at Redwoods Monastery reinforces this view. According to Brother David Steindl-Rast's recollection, Merton advised the Trappists to discover contemplative unity in their surroundings: "Enjoy this. Drink it all in. Everything, the redwood forest, the sea, the waves, the birds, the sea-lions. It is in all this that you will find your answers. Here is where everything connects."[30]

For Merton photography offers another way of praying, another path of merging inner and outer landscapes, another means of illustrating how "we and our world interpenetrate" and how landscape, nature, and indeed the whole world are "a living and self-creating mystery of which I am myself a part, to which I am myself my own unique door" (CWA, 151–52). Photography becomes another way to merge the mundane and the profound, another invitation to awaken the eye and the heart to new consciousness, another way to proclaim the "invisible fecundity" and "hidden wholeness" of all beings.

Published poems and photos continue to offer scholars opportunities for more sophisticated literary, theological, psychological, and thematic study, but here—against the backdrop of Merton's journals—they serve as benchmarks to illustrate how Merton's spiritual life is moving deeper into contemplation and mysticism, and how nature is a major inspiration and vehicle for his prayer. When Merton becomes the bobwhite in his poem about worship, or when he frames a photo of a tree against the misty horizon, he is plunging into matter and simultaneously into the Divine. Likewise, when he spends extended time at the hermitage, he is realizing more precisely how God is everywhere and how everywhere is home; he is experiencing the beauty and unity in nature that the eighteenth-century philosopher and theologian Jonathan Edwards called a "consent to being." Such discoveries lead naturally to experiences of healing and wholeness.

## Nature Offers Healing and Wholeness

As early as 1953, when Merton is seeking more solitude for prayer in the toolshed that he christens Saint Anne's, he notes in his journal how everything "real in me has come back to life in this doorway open to the sky! . . . Everything has come together in unity and the unity is not my unity but Yours, O Father of Peace." The silence of this makeshift hermitage, he asserts, "is making me well" (SS 32–33). Several years later, when Merton feels the strain of preparing conferences for the

novices, enduring chronic illness, and meeting writing deadlines, he
seeks the solace of the woods: "It was so good to get back and smell
the sweet air of the woods and listen to the silence" (SS 239). To re-
cuperate from the busy Christmas feast and lengthy liturgies, Merton
enjoys "sitting quietly under the frosty cedars and looking at the quiet
grey sky and breathing the clean air" (SS 240). Central to his journal
excerpts, crafted into *Conjectures of a Guilty Bystander,* is Merton's realization that his vow of stability—a promise to allow "place" to offer
the means to holiness—is deepening his commitment to the wilderness
and bringing him to a sense of home he has been longing for all his life.
Although cited in earlier chapters, several of these journal excerpts are
worth a second reading for their emphasis on healing and wholeness.
For example, once Merton is spending more prayer time in the Saint
Mary of Carmel hermitage, he indicates how focused and integrated
he feels:

> this is tremendous: with the tall pines, the silence, the moon and stars
> above the pines as dark falls, the patterns of shadow, the vast valley
> and hills everything speaks of a more mature and more complete
> solitude. The pines are tall and not low. There is frankly a house,
> demanding not attachment but responsibility. A silence for dedica-
> tion and not for escape. Lit candles in the dusk. *Haec requies mea in
> saeculum saeculi.* [This is my resting place forever]—the sense of a
> journey ended, of wandering at an end. *The first time in my life* I ever
> really felt I had come home and that my waiting and looking were
> ended (TTW 79–80; Merton's emphasis).

A couple of years later, after a short stay in the hospital for recurring
health problems, Merton again embraces his beloved woods. He relishes the "sense of recovery, of returning to something good and sane,
principally the quiet here. . . . I felt again, once more, a renewal of
the first intuition, the awareness of belonging where these rocky hills
are, that I belong to this parcel of land with pine trees and woods and
fields, and that this is my place" (TTW 244). In this passage, revised
for *Conjectures,* Merton more precisely sums it up: "I belong to this
parcel of land with rocky rills around it, with pine trees on it. These

are the woods and fields that I have worked in, and walked in, and in which I have encountered the deepest mystery of my own life. And in a sense I never chose this place for myself, it was chosen for me (though of course one must ratify the choice by a personal decision)" (CGB 257). Some time later, when he is spending occasional overnights in the hermitage, he elaborates on this deeper spiritual insight:

> Went to bed late at the hermitage. All quiet. No lights at Boone's or Newton's. Cold. Lay in bed realizing that what I was, was *happy*. Said the strange word "happiness" and realized that it was there, not as an "it" or object. It simply was. And I was that. And this morning, coming down, seeing the multitude of stars above the bare branches of the wood, I was suddenly hit, as it were, with the whole package of meaning of everything: that the immense mercy of God was upon me, that the Lord in infinite kindness had looked down on me and given me this vocation out of love, and that he had always intended this, and how foolish and trivial had been all my fears and twistings and desperation. And no matter what anyone else might do or say about it, however they might judge or evaluate it, all is irrelevant in the reality of my vocation to solitude, even though I am not a typical hermit. (DWL 177–78)

Merton's experience of open-air evenings and early morning dew reenacts the counsel of Mencius, the Chinese philosopher Merton had read in the 1950s (mentioned in chapter 3). In his Ox Mountain parable, Mencius, who believed human beings are essentially good, affirms the need for solitude, quiet, and regenerative, healing rest. Merton was attracted to the wisdom of Mencius, even writing a poetic version of the parable published in 1960 by Victor Hammer as a broadside and the next year in *Commonweal;* it was later included in *Mystics and Zen Masters* and *Collected Poems.* Merton notes in his journal in mid-1960 the "importance of 'night-spirit' and 'dawn-breath' in the restoration of the trees to life. Men cut them down, beasts browse on the new shoots, no night spirit and no dawn breath—no rest; no renewal—and then one is convinced at last that the mountain *never had* any trees on it" (TTW 19; Merton's emphasis). It is obvious that Merton gets the meaning of the parable: its application to human beings who are so much engaged in "doing" that they forget to be engaged in "being." In *Conjectures* Merton develops his insight on the need for a rhythm of life, so ingrained in the Benedictine tradition of work, prayer, and rest. He writes: "Without the night spirit, the dawn breath, silence, passivity, rest, man's nature cannot be itself. In its barrenness it is no longer *natura:* nothing grows from it, nothing is born of it any more" (CGB 137).

We can infer how influential Mencius and his guidelines for healing and wholeness are by noting that Merton locates his comments on the Ox Mountain parable in the center of *Conjectures,* even titling this pivotal chapter "The Night Spirit and the Dawn Air." Just as the solitary darkness has a restoring effect on Ox Mountain, so too does the hermitage solitude have a healing effect on Merton. As Paul Pearson notes in an introduction to Merton's poem about the Ox Mountain parable in *The Merton Annual,* Merton delights in the parable because it offers a different kind of wisdom than does the secular world: what Merton refers to as the "heart of a child" and a "parable of mercy."[31] This parable, asserts Pearson, gives expression to Merton's "experience of the effect nature has upon him, especially the effect of the woods and of nature in the very early hours of the morning, a time when he, as a Cistercian monk, is awake as nature itself begins to awaken. The understanding of nature that Merton finds in Mencius's parable fits into his own expression of "paradise consciousness" so that, in the early morning, Merton discovers "an unspeakable secret: paradise is all around us and we do not understand," the "dawn deacon" cries out "wisdom" but "we don't attend."[32] Once we realize the pervasiveness of paradise, once we realize we swim in an ocean of the mercy of God, our vision expands. As Pearson notes, Merton's "horizons had begun to broaden rapidly. The mercy he felt so strongly in Jonas led gradually to an overflowing of mercy and compassion toward others: beginning with those with whom he was in contact in the monastery, the scholastics and then novices, through his expanding correspondence, the stream of visitors who came to Gethsemani to see him and through his writings, especially his writings on the social issues of his day."³³ What Merton is also beginning to intuit, I propose, is a sense of the compassion and healing refreshment necessary for all nature.

Being privy to the sometimes capricious yet committed mind of Merton as revealed in his almost daily journal writing allows us to witness the complexity of his expanding vision, his desire for personal wholeness, and his escalating concern for social justice. His journals offer a kind of literary trajectory of his thinking and praying that help us understand why reading Rachel Carson's *Silent Spring* is a pivotal moment in his evolving consciousness. As Dennis Patrick O'Hara points out, there are certain touchstone moments in Merton's published writing that indicate important shifts in his thinking.³⁴ *Bread in the Wilderness* (1953), according to O'Hara, reveals an earlier theology that regards the fall of Adam and Eve as clouding the window of creation; *New Seeds of Contemplation* reveals a monk who believes that "in all created things we, who do not yet perfectly love God, can find something that reflects the fulfillment of heaven and something that reflects the anguish of hell" (NSC 26). Merton's letter to Rachel Carson, asserts O'Hara, reveals an even more favorable holistic theological position, namely, that the world itself is "a transparent manifestation of the love of God" (WF 71). Such discoveries, fostered by additional time spent in the woods, become the backdrop of Merton's ever-awakening, ever-stretching consciousness that embraces the integrity of God's creation and that enables him to declare boldly in his letter to Rachel Carson:

> The whole world itself, to religious thinkers, has always appeared as a transparent manifestation of the love of God, as a "paradise" of His wisdom, manifested in all His creatures, down to the tiniest, and in the most wonderful interrelationship between them. Man's vocation was to be in this cosmic creation, so to speak, as the eye in the body. What I say now is a religious, not a scientific statement. That is to say, man is at once a part of nature and he transcends it. In maintaining this delicate balance, he must make use of nature wisely, and understand his position, ultimately relating both himself and visible

nature to the invisible—in my terms, to the Creator, in any case, to the source and exemplar of all being and all life. (WF 71)

This public declaration reveals yet another turning point in Merton's spirituality. In the words of Robinson Jeffers, a poet he respected, Merton was discovering more deeply that the "universe is one being, all its parts are different expressions of the same energy, and they are all in communication with each other, . . . therefore parts of an organic whole. . . . It seems to me that this whole alone is worthy of the deeper sort of love."[35] Merton's commitment to being awake, his ability to respond to grace-filled extraordinary moments as well as ordinary experiences, and his ongoing love affair with all aspects of nature that he found so life-giving—"the silence of the forest is my bride and the sweet dark warmth of the whole world is my love" (DWL 240)— prepare him for his "turning toward the world" and his commitment to social justice. But Merton is also beginning to regard ecological justice as part of his personal responsibility, a widening of what Thomas Berry calls our "identification horizon."[36] By being true to his Benedictine heritage to listen with the ear of the heart, and by learning to see differently and study carefully the spirituality of Cistercian luminaries and other writers, Merton has come to incorporate into his own life Bernard of Clairvaux's wisdom: "You will find something more in woods than in books. Trees and stones will teach you that which you can never learn from masters."[37]

# Chapter 6

# Merton's Evolving
# Ecological Consciousness

> In a sense, a very true and solitary sense, coming to the hermit-
> age has been a "return to the world," not a return to the cities,
> but a return to direct and humble contact with God's world,
> His creation, and the world of poor men who work.
> —Thomas Merton, *Dancing in the Water of Life*

Merton biographers, as well as multiple Merton scholars, have clearly documented the late 1950s and early 1960s as Merton's "turning
toward the world." His moment of epiphany in March 1958 while
crossing the busy intersection of Fourth and Walnut streets in Louisville attests to the beginning of this turning. No longer does Merton
believe he can "hide" in the monastery to work out his personal salvation; no longer does he regard a monastic vocation as something
separate and apart from the world; Merton now understands in a new
experiential way that *contemptus mundi* (rejection of the world) is a
flawed theology. All human beings are connected, and therefore matter matters. And as Belden Lane accurately comments about Merton's monastic experience, "True contemplation . . . has to reenter
the world of others with its newly won freedom . . . and the exercise
of a compassion whose shape is justice."[1] For Merton, John Donne's
seventeenth-century meditation "No Man Is an Island" takes on deeper meaning—even becoming the title for Merton's mid-1950s book
on community and Christian tradition;[2] and the naturalist John Muir's
oft-quoted 1911 insight that each creature is "hitched to everything

else in the Universe" brings Merton to an even more mature and inclusive vision.[3] These years are also a time of increased publications. *Disputed Questions* (September 1960), *The Wisdom of the Desert* (April 1961), *Hagia Sophia* (January 1962), *The New Man* (January 1962), *New Seeds of Contemplation* (January 1962), and *Original Child Bomb* (March 1962) have been occupying Merton's thinking and writing time. Furthermore, his unpublished Working Notebooks reveal wide and eclectic reading, as he is delving into works by poets, novelists, anthropologists, philosophers, theologians, psychologists, and medieval mystics.[4]

Amazingly, considering the little time a monastic *horarium* allows for these activities, Merton is also in correspondence with James Forest and Gordon Zahn, nonviolence and peace advocates; the literary and cultural figures Boris Pasternak, Pablo Antonio Cuadra, Czesław Miłosz, Miguel Grinberg, and Lawrence Ferlinghetti; and such various religious notables as Doña Luisa Coomaraswamy, Abdul Aziz, Edward Deming Andrews, Abraham Heschel, Louis Massignon, and D. T. Suzuki.[5] This wide spectrum of contacts illustrates Merton's expanding knowledge about world events and offers him a venue for speaking out on a host of religious and social issues. Although forbidden by his Trappist superiors to publish essays against war and the proliferation of weapons, Merton creates an alternative avenue of communication about the horrors and futility of war through a series of mimeographed Cold War letters written between October 1961 and October 1962 and sent far and wide to friends around the world.[6]

As Victor Kramer astutely acknowledges in his introduction to volume 4 of the journals, aptly titled *Turning toward the World*, Merton is engaged in a "systematic drawing together and examination" of his place in and responsibility to the world, revealing a mind aware of and engaging the urgent questions facing contemporary culture. *Conjectures of a Guilty Bystander* (1966), which is a substantial reworking of his journal ruminations and preoccupations during this opening-up period, "demonstrates Merton's renewed energy in the early 1960s and his emergent openness to questions not just about himself, but about monastic relationships to other religious traditions, art, architecture, and the Church, as well as about society at large, especially issues concerning race, war, nuclear madness, and other basic threats to civilization as a whole." Kramer accurately notes that Merton's current interest in greater solitude coincides with "a renewed awakening to nature, the beauty of the landscape, the wonder of a particular moment." Volume 4 of the journals reveals a "developing awe, celebration, and praise" of both humans and nature that documents Merton's "movement from cloister toward world, from Novice Master to hermit, and from ironic critic of culture to compassionate singer of praise."[7]

It should not be surprising, then, that after reading *Silent Spring,* Merton feels compelled to write to Rachel Carson. Though chapter 1 of this text focuses on the literary and conceptual resonances between Carson and Merton, which were based on their parallel training in awareness, there are embedded in Merton's letter deep theological insights about human responsibility, compassion, and justice that reveal his expanding ecological consciousness. The very structure of his letter suggests the process of his thinking. He first compliments Carson, then suggests the existence of a macro problem, attempting to name its essence and reasons for its spread. He cites flaws in human logic, our responsibility to seek a remedy, and his affirmation of love of nature. Let us take a second look at this letter to follow more precisely his line of thinking (WF 70–72).

In his opening paragraph Merton not only articulates his praise for Carson's work, but also acknowledges its wider, even cosmic, significance. By noting that her writing is "more timely even than you or I realize," Merton is suggesting that Carson has implicitly identified an issue broader than technology as the source of our troubles. She has engaged in "the diagnosis of the ills of our civilization." Merton tries to articulate what those ills might be. He cites our pattern of behavior that uses "titanic power" to focus on minute problems while not only missing the big picture, but denying as well the far-reaching and negative effects of our futile attempts to eradicate a problem.

Already Merton is alluding to a deep belief in the interconnectedness of all creation, what John Muir frequently referred to as the "web of life." Our scorn for micro annoyances, insists Merton, mirrors our scorn for life itself. Small troubles are reflective of larger tribulations and must be seen, as well as responded to, in light of their planetary dimensions. By not being able to recognize this pattern, we fall into the fallacy of treating symptoms that only "aggravate the sickness: *the remedies are expressions of the sickness itself*" (Merton's emphasis). Merton boldly names our illness a "dreadful hatred of life." Caught in "superficial optimism" and "materialistic affluence" that are "ultimately self-defeating," modern humanity is trapped by "built-in frustrations" that lead to "despair in the midst of 'plenty' and 'happiness'" and ultimately to "indiscriminate, irresponsible destructiveness." Merton sums up his analysis with a telling observation: "In order to 'survive' we instinctively destroy that on which our survival depends."

Where does this tendency originate? Merton suggests that whether or not we subscribe to the Genesis explanation of the Fall, our human frailty, borne out by "mythical and poetic expression," seems bent on destroying what is good. Merton then articulates a personal credo he shares with religious mystics from multiple traditions: "The whole world itself, to religious thinkers, has always appeared as a transparent manifestation of the love of God, as a 'paradise' of His wisdom, manifested in all His creatures, down to the tiniest, and in the wonderful interrelationship between them." In one sentence, Merton capsulizes the essence of incarnational thinking: because the Divine in its unending creativity has inserted itself into life on Earth, everything that is, is holy; the divine spark dwells in all creatures; consequently, each being is related to and interdependent with every other being.

The deeply planted seeds of Merton's keen awareness of nature and his growing sense of justice, as illustrated in his journals, letters, and public writing, emerge in the second half of the letter. Humans are not only "part of nature," he writes, but a transcendent part that has responsibility for the voiceless. Merton even elevates this responsibility beyond duty to a unique "vocation"—a call to be in "this cosmic creation . . . as the eye in the body," a role that commissions humans to "make use of nature wisely, and understand [our] position, ultimately relating" all human and nonhuman nature "to the Creator, in any case, to the source and exemplar of all being and all life."

Strong words from a monk who has just read a book about the terrible effects of DDT. But Merton, through a lifetime of being awake to and aware of his surroundings, is astute at making philosophical leaps and existential connections. Like the raven of Native lore, he is one who "speaks strong words." His growing sense of social justice, his reservations about the potentially dehumanizing effects of technology, and his commitment to nonviolence lead him naturally and gracefully to create a poignant analogy: frantic attempts to eradicate the Japanese beetle—to view it as "Other" without regard for the ramifications on civilization and life itself—are linked to our ongoing fascination with nuclear war and obsession with the Viet Cong. Yet Merton is not a single-issue social critic. He acknowledges that technology and wisdom are not essentially opposed, and that the challenge of our age is "to unite them in a supreme humility which will result in a totally self-forgetful creativity and service" that supports all life on the planet. We are challenged to move beyond hubris to humility. Three years before he comes to read about it, Merton is articulating an insight close to the conservationist Aldo Leopold's principle for forming an ecological conscience: "A thing is right when it tends to preserve the integrity, stability, and beauty of the biotic community. It is wrong when it tends otherwise."[8]

We might look at Carson and Merton's viewpoint this way. Imagine a horizontal continuum whose endpoints represent ecocentrism and egocentrism (or anthropocentrism), a visual measure of our attitude toward the position and power of human beings in the universe. Imagine, too, a vertical continuum whose endpoints represent principles of community and commodity, a visual measure of our attitude toward nonhuman creation.

Both Carson, in her careful research for *Silent Spring*, and Merton, in his response to her provocative text, are sensing the arrogance of humanity, which believes it can act on whatever it learns from science or technology. Intellectual breakthroughs and scientific discoveries equal human progress. An ethic of "could we, therefore should we?" does not exist. A corollary to this view is how nonhuman nature is to be valued. Sadly, there seems to be little recognition of *bonum* (that which

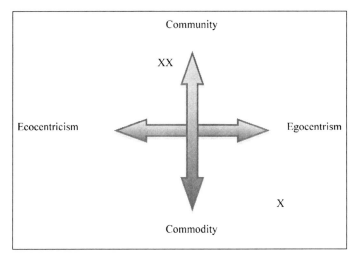

Our place in creation (horizontal) and our attitude toward nonhuman nature (vertical).

has inherent value and dignity) in nonhuman nature and heavy emphasis on *utilitas* (that which is practical and useful). Nonhuman nature is valued only so far as it is useful to humankind; there is little recognition or consideration of our interdependence with creation, and therefore no respect for the rights of any other created being. Certainly there is no acknowledgment of any communion between human and nonhuman beings, and no thought of making decisions based on a planetary principle that the theologian Elaine Prevallet calls "in the service of life." Indeed, Prevallet has recently cited our essential human failing as separating ourselves "from appropriate participation in the larger life process. When [humans] indulge their own comfort or entertainment or curiosity without considering the effect upon the rest of the earth family, humans violate their own human being, for in fact they can exist only within a *relationship of reciprocity* with the rest. In Christian terminology, we call that sin, which in fact leads to our own demise."[9]

If we were to graph Carson and Merton's view of the catastrophic tensions engulfing government, technology, science, and local decision makers, we would need to place an "X" in the lower far-right quadrant of the grid: using their "titanic power" and "awful irresponsibility" to wipe out all perceived enemies, they thus endanger life itself. What Carson and Merton are calling us to, however, is a rethinking of our place as human beings and a transformation of our attitude toward nonhuman nature. *Silent Spring* and Merton's affirmation of its accurate view of the ills of contemporary society challenge humankind to see itself, as Merton says, as "a part of nature," to respond to the call "to be in this cosmic creation, so to speak, as the eye in the body"; man (and woman) must "make use of nature wisely, and understand his position, ultimately relating both himself and visible nature to the invisible—in my terms, to the Creator, in any case, to the source and exemplar of all being and all life." Carson and Merton would have us transform our thinking to recognize our special role as human beings responsible for nurturing and supporting the community of life to which we belong and of which we are a special part. They would have us think and act in such a way that we might be worthy of the position in the upper inner left quadrant of the graph (××).

Embedded in Merton's letter to Rachel Carson are three strands of his deepening spirituality: awareness and a keen eye for the beauty and the holiness or "sacramentality" of nature, a deepening realization of our kinship and harmony with nature, and a growing sense of compassion and responsibility for all creation. These strands, as we have seen in previous chapters, are seeds sown and watered in Merton's childhood fascination with nature, in his epiphanic experiences, as well as in his recognition of the holy in the ordinariness of life and in his facility for allowing prayer to merge both outer and inner landscapes of his experience. Taken together and gaining more prominence in his praying and writing over the years, these strands braid themselves in the 1960s into a new and evolving ecological vision. This emerging vision is both the impetus for Merton's letter to Rachel Carson and the backdrop for his subsequent letters and book reviews in the final months before his untimely death on December 10, 1968, in Bangkok, Thailand. Although we have looked at these strands individually in a somewhat biographical way, we can also discern how they become part of the fabric of Merton's spirituality particularly in the last years of his life.

## A Keen Eye for Nature's Beauty

*[handwritten marginal note: John! the word became flesh]*

Despite his emphasis on social justice issues during the late 1950s and into the 1960s, Merton never loses his propensity for seeing beauty and feeling excitement in the materiality of nature and expressing this fascination with poetic lyricism. His celebration of light, landscape, woods, and the critters in them continues as one strong strand of his incarnational spirituality. Readers of his journals, especially volumes 4, 5, and 6, are treated to multiple picturesque descriptions that pop up everywhere. No burning social crisis, business in the monastery, or summary of new reading materials completely distracts Merton from noticing and rejoicing in his surroundings. In addition to periodic weather reports, elegant images like these dance across the pages: "White smoke rising up in the valley, against the light, slowly taking animal forms, with a dark background of wooded hills behind" (TTW 73); "During Chapter (in library) a kingfisher flew through the *préau* [courtyard in front of the monastery]—a blue flash outside a window, and then the rattle of his controlled excitement" (TTW 41); "Here you can really *watch* a storm. White snakes of lightning suddenly stand in the sky and vanish" (TTW 107); "Tiny, delicate fishbones of clouds in the sky. Harps of sound in the sweet trees" (DWL 143); "Redbuds still blooming and Dogwoods coming out into full bloom like constellations in the green gloom of pines" (LL 214); "A fine clear silent night. During meditation—listening to the vast silent coldness and sleep of woods and awakeness of stars" (LL 295). Merton's ability to *see* illustrates his belief in the inherent value of nature's materiality. For Merton nature is both means and end. Its innate goodness gives rise to what recent scholarship has termed an "ecology of humility"— a reverential awe and desire to preserve nature's beauty in the face of mystery that is larger than humankind.[10]

## Kinship and Harmony with Nature

Merton's love of nature, however, goes beyond delighting in it merely as a spectrum of color and light. During this period he more frequently and more deeply senses his connection with other living beings. For example, in recounting his pleasure in praying the Divine Office in the woods at the break of dawn (July 9, 1961), Merton asserts how he is "in harmony with all the singing birds under the bright sky." Ancient prayers such as Psalm 65, celebrating the overflowing pastures of the wilderness, the hills encircled with joy, and the valleys clothed with flocks, play out before him. He is moved to exclaim: "Everything you have on your lips in praising God is there before you—hills, dew, light, birds, growing things" (TTW 140). Or as he rephrases this comment for the published version in *Conjectures*: "Praise reaches not only the heart of God but also the heart of creation itself, finding everywhere the beauty of the righteousness of Yahweh" (CGB 137).

Such kinship with nature prompts Merton to admit he is "part of the weather and part of the climate and part of the place" (TTW 299–300); moreover, he asserts he is more fully human when he lives "with the tempo of the sun and of the day, in harmony with what is around me" (DWL 146). This awareness of relationship with nature enables Merton to take pleasure in a flock of playful myrtle warblers (now officially identified as magnolia warblers) feeding in the conifers just above his head. "I was awed at their loveliness, their quick flight, their hissings and chirpings, the yellow spot on the back revealed in flight, etc. Sense of total kinship with them as if they and I were of the same nature, and as if that nature were nothing but love. And what else but love keeps us all together in being?" (DWL 162). On another occasion he remarks on how calm the towhees and tanagers are when he is at the hermitage. "It is a wonderful companionship to have them constantly within the very small circle of woods which is their area and mine—where they have their nests and I have mine" (DWL 245). Surely, with his ongoing study of sacred scripture and his commitment to contemplative living, Merton is sensing the ultimate unity and interdependence of all being, solemnized and made holy by the incarnate Jesus, who, as Saint Paul writes, is "the firstborn of all creation," in whom "all things hold together" (Colossians 1:15–17).

Notably, the deer in the woods behind the hermitage are cause for realizing harmony with creation. Enchanted by their mysterious silence, their big ears and inquiring eyes, and their quiet gazing, Merton often feels related to them. With a "contemplative intuition" he senses that the deer "reveals to me something essential in myself! Something beyond the trivialities of my everyday being, and my individuality." Elated by the deer's unique inscape and ancient Spirit that fascinated artists of early cave paintings, Merton admits he longs to touch them (DWL 189, 291). Such experiences also help him be aware of how much the out-of-doors landscape influences his inner landscape: "I love the woods, particularly around the hermitage. Know every tree, every animal, every bird. Sense of relatedness to my environment—a luxury I refuse to renounce. Aristocrat, conservative: I don't give a damn. Those city Christians can live in their world of Muzak and $CO_2$ and think they are in touch with 'creation'—nature 'humanism'! I admit that it is a reality one must acknowledge but am not so sure it is better for self-confrontation" (LL 208).

These multiple experiences of harmony and kinship coincide with Merton's reading of Teilhard de Chardin's groundbreaking study of scientific evolution, *The Divine Milieu*—and perhaps elicit this brief journal comment: "Real importance of Teilhard—his affirmation of the 'holiness of matter'" (DWL 260). In an essay entitled "The Universe as Epiphany," Merton agrees with Teilhard that a *"disincarnate or disembodied"* Christianity is a false understanding of Christianity; he affirms Teilhard's belief in "the 'divine milieu' which surrounds, sustains, and embraces [us] all together in harmony and in unity."[11] Although in a second essay, "Teilhard's Gamble," Merton expresses reservations about Teilhard's focus on the evolutionary supremacy of humans, which seems to ignore the "wounds of mendacity and hatred" that have been deepened by "technological warfare, totalitarianism, and genocide," he is nevertheless willing to compliment Teilhard on his belief in the "fundamental oneness" of all creation and his hope in a new religious consciousness.[12]

## Learning Responsibility and Compassion

A third strand of Merton's evolving ecological consciousness that is becoming more clear in his thinking and writing is revealed poignantly in the centerpiece of his letter to Carson when he underscores our transcendent position in nature and our concomitant responsibility to "make use of nature wisely." It is not enough to celebrate nature and revel in harmony with it; human beings are called to act justly toward all creation. The prophet Micah's counsel "to act justly, love tenderly, and walk humbly with your God" (Micah 6:8) is more than a trio of catchphrases about loving God and neighbor. The prophetic witness for right relationships that Merton has been so immersed in during the late 1950s and early 1960s, he comes to believe, encompasses more than justice toward humans. This sense of planetary justice does not, however, emerge out the blue. Awakening to the immanent presence of the "holy" leads to deeper compassion with all our brothers and sisters, both human and nonhuman. Put in other words, Merton's aesthetic response to the beauty of his landscape moves toward ethical response and a cry for justice. As Judith Plant, an ecofeminist, has observed, once we have felt "the life of the other," we arrive at a "new starting point for human decision making."[13] Merton's letter to Rachel Carson signals just such a new starting point, one in a series of transformations that make Merton an early spokesman for environmental responsibility.

Even before Merton writes his letter to Rachel Carson, there are inklings in his early activity and writing that he was beginning to develop a take on ecological responsibility. In the 1950s Merton not only was interested in being a monastery forest ranger, but was also involved in simple conservation activism to control erosion on the monastery grounds. After requesting hundreds of loblolly pine seedlings from the government, Merton, with the assistance of the novices, was responsible for reforesting whole sections of the Gethsemani property. Such initiative suggests Merton's concern for the Earth before environmental consciousness had become widespread and trendy. Brother Patrick Hart, one of those tree-planting novices and later Merton's secretary, recounts that Merton regarded the woods as a "sacrament of God's presence and was concerned about preserving it not only for our generation, but for the generations to come." Merton saw in the growth of these seedlings a symbolic parallelism between "all growing things" and the "young monks who were entrusted to him."[14]

In June 1952 Merton generates a long journal entry laying out his philosophy about nature. In this almost seven-page entry, Merton acknowledges how much he loves Gethsemani, how he enjoys saying Mass for the lay brothers, and how he takes pleasure in his "private dawn," at which he can be "silent with God." He quotes his favorite psalm (Psalm 83 in the old numbering; 84 in modern notation) about nests for sparrows and blessings for all who dwell in God's house; he rhapsodizes about how God, who "owns all things, leaves them all to themselves. . . . His love is unpossessive," and thus the "grasses grow where they will," the "stars serve Him freely," the "sun rises with a song of joy," and "the clean gentle speechless moon goes down to her bed without protest." But, Merton laments, we human beings, in our brokenness and penchant for possessing things, will never truly praise God until we learn to respect the integrity of each item of creation" (ES 471–77). This passage becomes another seed that in silence, contemplation, and interaction with the woods comes to full bloom in Merton's later years.

Though I have insisted that Merton's letter to Rachel Carson is a watershed moment in the evolution of his ecological consciousness, his transformation in thinking is not automatic, nor is it complete. Even after his January 1963 admission to Carson that he had used DDT in the past, Merton has much to learn. A mere three months later he is aghast at his own compliance in dealing death to creation. Having enjoyed the "beautiful whistling of titmice," he discovers one dead near the hermitage, realizing that the calcium chloride applied to anthills may have been responsible for the bird's demise. Merton confides in his journal: "What a miserable bundle of foolish idiots we are! We kill everything around us even when we think we love and respect nature and life. This sudden power to deal death all around us *simply by the way we live* . . . is by far the most disturbing symptom of our time. . . . A phenomenal number of species of animals and birds have *become extinct* in the last fifty years—due of course to man's irruption into ecology" (TTW 312; Merton's emphasis). During this same time, when Merton is reading about the history of Zen Buddhism, one of several topics of interest to him, his Working Notebook 11 contains a comment about how Chinese Zen Buddhism emphasizes harmony with nature.[15]

In November 1964 he celebrates birds and critters in his natural environment, but he is dismayed at the carnage he creates in killing a wasp. Merton waxes eloquent about the titmouse "swinging and playing in the dry weeds by the woodshed," the quail "whistling in the field by the hermitage," and the diminutive shrew that "ran a little on to my sleeve and then stayed fixed, trembling" until he released her outside. Then comes the downside of this episode: "But what of the wasp in the hermitage that I killed with insecticide? I was shocked to find it an hour later in great agony. It would have been simpler to kill it with the flyswatter" (DWL 161). Here we see Merton falling short of the Buddhist principle of *ahimsa* ("do no harm"), but at least realizing that creatures are not commodities to be disposed of at will with a convenient chemical. Acknowledging the violence of his action creates another opportunity for becoming awake. As the Buddhist scholar Joanna Macy has recently written: "The most remarkable feature of this historical moment on Earth is not that we are on the way to destroying the world—we've actually been on the way for quite a while. It is that we are beginning to wake up, as from a millennia-long sleep, to a whole new relationship to our world, to ourselves and each other. This is the great and necessary adventure of our time."[16] Although Merton is not yet completely transformed, he is learning; he is embracing the great and necessary adventure. And his steps toward conversion and a more mature sense of environmental responsibility are worth chronicling because they contribute to a crescendo of intensity that culminates in a final book review published during the summer before his death.

During this same period of the mid-1960s, another healing and invigorating event offers Merton reassurance that his desire to live in the woods in kinship with nature is not just a selfish or idiosyncratic whim: Merton comes in contact with Celtic spirituality. On June 2, 1964, for example, Merton refers in his journal to "a new world that has waited until this time to open up" (DWL 107). During subsequent weeks, both Merton's journal and his Working Notebook 14 indicate how charmed he is by Celtic nature poetry, its reverence for the raven as a symbol of second sight, and the ancient legends of

Saint Columba's and Saint Brendan's nautical journeys. He finds the *Navigatio S. Brendani* a symbol for the "earthly paradise the ultimate ideal," and its reliance on Celtic myth "a hook on which to hang a manifesto of spiritual renewal in the monastic life" (DWL 128, 131). Part of Merton's fascination with Celtic lore can be traced to his Welsh heritage on his father's side, but its allure goes beyond genetics. Merton, who has become so comfortable in the company of creatures, is captivated by the Celtic threefold understandings still embraced today in the ecumenical community at Iona, Scotland: the importance of a "deep sense of connectedness" to God, to the sacred Earth, and to each other. Committed to this trinity of right relationships, human beings are called to celebrate and preserve the integrity of creation because creation is a window onto the Divine. If one is awake, aware, the "thin spaces," or the margins between the natural and the supernatural worlds, afford opportunities to savor the outrageous bounty of God and recognize the powerful presence of the Holy Spirit. Prayer and praise arise out of the experiences of daily living and the Divine is revealed in the ordinary events of life. According to Celtic thinking, *this* time and *this* place are sacred: now and here are where God abides, calling us to live with a sense of wonder.[17] The Scottish Episcopalian theologian John Macquarrie has phrased it well: "At the very centre of this type of spirituality was an intense sense of presence. The Celt was very much a God-intoxicated man whose life was embraced on all sides by the Divine Being. But this presence was always mediated through some finite, this-world reality, so that it would be difficult to imagine a spirituality more down to earth than this one."[18] Somehow, without specific reference to a particular Trappist monk, Macquarrie's description of a God-intoxicated individual grounded in nature seems to fit Thomas Merton.

Immersing himself in Kenneth Jackson's *Studies in Early Celtic Nature Poetry* and other texts on Celtic lore, Merton not only copies passages about the direct influence of a solitary life in the wilderness on the creation of ancient Irish poetry, but understands his own hermitage experience as a reflection or reenactment of early Celtic monks. In his Working Notebook 14 Merton rejoices in the similarity he perceives between the ancient hermits and his life in the woods. From Jackson's text he copies out this sentence: "The solitary hermitage in the wilderness, the life of rustic purity and humble poetry, the spare diet of herbs and water, are the distinguishing marks of rich Irish poetry."[19] His subsequent notes comment on this ancient immersion in the wilderness: "The ultimate significance of the hermit's relationship with nature is something that transcends both nature and hermit alike. . . . Bird and hermit are joining together in an act of worship; the very existence of nature was a song of praise in which he himself took part by entering into harmony with nature."[20] How understandable this would be to Merton. So many times Kentucky birds and one Gethsemani hermit had joined in worship, causing Merton to revel in nature and to be nourished by it, especially when reciting Lauds in the woods with a predawn avian chorus.

Merton regards his ongoing fascination with and investigation of Celtic monasticism and Celtic poetry as de facto affirmation of his call both to live in harmony with his woodland landscape and to recognize the paradoxical danger and promise of solitude. His journal reflection for his fiftieth birthday (January 31, 1965) acknowledges that danger in nautical imagery, when "the ropes are cast off and the skiff is no longer tied to land" (DWL 200); in a Working Notebook entry for this same date Merton copies out reassuring advice from medieval Mechtilde of Magdeburg:

> "No Thing" your love must be
> And from that "Thing" you must flee.
> You must stand alone
> With no man make your home . . .
> So will your dwelling
> Be wilderness.

Merton, the man of paradox, is attracted to Celtic spirituality and its awareness of the "thin places" where the supernatural manifests itself; he also knows himself to be particularly adept at living on the border between the monastery and the hermitage, embracing the spirituality of both the West and the East, comfortable with the monastic traditions of silence and the necessity of speaking out on issues of social justice. Such ability for living on the edge or border between two nourishing environments or ecosystems—what environmental writers call the ecotone—is both promise and danger. The edge of any landscape offers nourishing options for local critters who inhabit the underbrush, yet it simultaneously presents the risk of exposure to encroaching predators.[21] Merton both recognizes and embraces this paradox, even composing in one of his Working Notebooks a "Text for an Office of Hermits," which presumably he anticipated using in the hermitage.[22]

In January 1965, in casual conversation with Illtud Evans, a British retreat master staying at the monastery, Merton learns there are now environmental protections in place on the Hebrides Islands; only those "protecting the wildlife and trying to restore the original ecology" are permitted to live on the island of Rum. Merton's journal comment is revealing: "This is wonderful!" (DWL 195). By Holy Week that year, as he is meditating on the ultimate obedience of Jesus to death on a cross, Merton is also reflecting on the broader environmental responsibility of all Christians. On Holy Thursday he writes: "Perhaps the most crucial aspect of Christian obedience to God today concerns the responsibility of the Christian in technological society toward God's creation and God's will for His creation. Obedience to God's will for nature and for man—respect for nature and love for man—in the awareness of our power to frustrate God's designs for nature and for man—to radically corrupt and destroy natural goods by misuse and blind exploitation, especially by criminal waste. The problem of nuclear war is only one facet of an immense, complex and unified problem" (DWL 227–28). On June 8, 1965, he is continuing to ponder the deep meaning of the greater solitude he feels called to. He writes in his journal: "The great joy of the solitary life is not found simply in quiet, in the beauty and peace of nature, song of birds etc., nor in the peace of one's own heart, but in the awakening and attuning of the heart to the voice of God. . . . It is not simply a question of 'existing' alone, but of doing, with joy and understanding 'the work of the cell' which is done in silence . . . in obedience to God" (DWL 254–55). In Notebook 17, after moving permanently to the hermitage that August, he writes: "I am here to learn to face death as my birth. . . . Here, planted as a seed in the cosmos, I will be a *Christ* seed, and bring fruit for other men."[23]

Perhaps all this concurrent reading and reflecting on Celtic spirituality is why his 1965 essay on his "day in the life of a monk," written at the request of Venezuelan poet Ludovico Silva, is so imbued with an ecological relationship with nature. Extended periods of contemplation in the hermitage enable Merton to understand not only that "the silence of the forest is [his] bride" but also that he is intimate with the environment around him. "I know there are trees here. I know there are birds here. I know the birds in fact very well . . . we form an ecological balance" (DWL 239–40). Merton includes in his journal notes—after a snapshot description of physical and mental ecology in the hermitage—a significant paragraph about non-ecology. Unfortunately, the revised and published version in *Day of a Stranger* omits this section wrung from his sensitive and responsive heart:

> There is also the non-ecology, the destructive unbalance of nature, poisoned and unsettled by bombs, by fallout, by exploitation: the land ruined, the waters contaminated, the soil charged with chemicals, ravaged with machinery, the houses of farmers falling apart because everybody goes to the city and stays there. . . . There is no poverty so great as that of the prosperous, no wretchedness so dismal as affluence. Wealth is poison. There is no misery to compare with that which exists where technology has been a total success. I know these are hard sayings, and that they are unbearable when they are said in other countries where so many lack everything. But do you imagine that if you become as prosperous as the United States you will no longer have needs? Here the needs are even greater. Full bellies have not brought peace and satisfaction but dementia, and in any case not all the bellies are full either. But the dementia is the same for all. (DWL 240)

Following this reproof of the evils caused by our human insanity—a list that loosely echoes the chapter organization of Carson's *Silent*

*Spring*—Merton makes his Thoreauvean declaration: "I live in the woods out of necessity." With personal testimony he elaborates how important are the dawn and the silence of the forest, and how he has "an obligation to preserve the stillness, the silence, the poverty, the virginal point of pure nothingness which is at the center of all other loves. I cultivate this plant silently in the middle of the night and water it with psalms and prophecies in silence. It becomes the most beautiful of all the trees in the garden" (DWL 240).

Merton's concern for ecological balance surfaces again after he has read a "good article" on ecology in *Daedalus,* and then a month later it turns to dismay when his early morning prayer is interrupted by squirrel hunters: "The woods all around crackle with guerrilla warfare. . . . In their mad way they love the woods too: but I wish their way were less destructive and less of a lie" (DWL 274, 283). In December he lists environmental problems, garnered as "news" from a neighbor, Andy Boone (DWL 323–24), and by early 1966 Merton is so taken with our twofold response-ability and responsibility for nature that he is convinced our mission is to "feel the spring. . . . The earth cannot *feel* all this. We must. But living away from the earth and the trees we fail them. We are absent from the wedding feast" (LL 19).

## Ecological Consciousness—Going Public

Merton's gradual process of transformation is evident in his journals and notebooks, but his letters and published book reviews during the last five years of his life reveal an urgency to share his broadening vision in a public venue. These letters and book reviews document an evolving and more intensely felt commitment to environmental integrity—a new consciousness motivated by justice for all creatures. A year after Merton's letter to Rachel Carson, for example, when he is perhaps still reflecting on her challenge to all Americans, Merton writes a charming, informal letter to Jim Frost, a high school sophomore from Waterloo, Iowa, who had asked Merton for a short note on his views on current issues. In addition to mentioning the importance of valuing life as a "good and a wonderful gift" and asserting that reality "is better than any illusion," Merton shares with this lad his delight in living in the woods and counting, the previous evening, at least five deer in his field: "It is wonderful to have wild animals for neighbors, and it is a shame that people can't think of anything better than to go and shoot them." Merton closes his letter with the "lesson" he wants young Jim to learn: "we Americans ought to love our land, our forests, our plains, and we ought to do everything we can to preserve it in its richness and beauty, by respect for our natural resources, for water, for land, for wild life. We need men and women of the rising generation to dedicate themselves to this" (RJ 330).

This theme of respect for natural resources and the urgent need to consider the ramifications of decisions emerges again in Merton's brief correspondence with Walter James, Lord Northbourne, a promoter of organic farming and author of *Religion in the Modern World*.[24] Merton respectfully disagrees with Northbourne on some points of his book, but they are in agreement over the as yet unidentified "implications of the technological revolution." Both liberal and conservative voices among the participants of Vatican Council II, writes Merton, are taking a "too superficial view of 'the world' "; in light of the H-bomb and our ability to exterminate civilization, "to speak with bland optimism of the future of man and of the Church blessing a new technological paradise becomes not only absurd but blasphemous. Yet at the same time, this technological society still has to be redeemed and sanctified in some way, not simply cursed and abhorred" (WF 312–14). Similar concern for the integrity of nature and the dangers of technology surfaces in Merton's brief correspondence with the poet and naturalist Gary Snyder, who, dividing his time between the Sierra Nevadas and Zen training in Japan, was writing forcefully about the beauty and intrinsic value of the natural environment.[25]

About the same time, Merton is reading George H. Williams's *Wilderness and Paradise in Christian Thought* and Ulrich W. Mauser's *Christ in the Wilderness*. In addition to multiple notes in his Working Notebook 24, several journal entries comment on Williams's "pleasing passion for the wilderness" and "his deep sense of importance, spiritually, of conservationism." Unlike his reaction to Rachel Carson,

Merton's response to Williams is that he is only "strongly tempted" to write to him (LL 158, 161). Apparently he never acts on this impulse. In his review of these two books, first published in *Cistercian Studies* in January 1967, Merton agrees with these Protestant scholars on the necessity of desert and wilderness for contemplation, then uses this opportunity—as he does in most book reviews—to draw a practical lesson for his primarily monastic audience. Merton writes: "If the monk is a man whose whole life is built around a deeply religious appreciation of his call to wilderness and paradise, and thereby to a special kind of kinship with God's creatures . . . and if technological society is constantly encroaching upon and destroying the remaining 'wildernesses' . . . [then monks] would seem to be destined by God, in our time, to be not only dwellers in the wilderness but also its protectors." To this telling paragraph Merton adds a footnote in which he muses that it "would be interesting to develop this idea" because hermits have a "natural opportunity" to act as forest rangers or fire guards in "our vast forests of North America."[26]

Curiously, yet perhaps not so curiously, Merton is connecting his early duties on fire watch and his unofficial position in the 1950s as forest ranger with his current reading, prayer, and recommitment to life in the woods. If, as he says, "this life in the woods is IT . . . that it is the life that has chosen itself for me" (LL 342), then being "married to the silence of the forest" carries with it additional responsibility to nurture and preserve it. The luxury of relatedness that he "refuse[s] to renounce" (LL 208) is consistent with not only contemplation in the wilderness but also responsibility for it.

This more inclusive ecological vision motivates Merton two days later (March 25, 1967) to confidently write a long letter to Mario Falsina, an Italian graduate student who had inquired about his views of the world. Merton numbers his comments from one to six, touching on the inherent goodness and sacramentality of the world, Marxism, his own conversion, contemporary evils of war and social injustice, influential Italian writers, and advice for young people. His response begins with a credo that the world is "God's good creation" and that Merton has "the good fortune to live in close contact with nature," where "God manifests himself in his creation, and everything that he has made speaks of him. . . . The world in itself can never be evil." Nevertheless, Merton cautions, despite being the "summit of God's creation," we can damage our intended relationship with creation. When "individuals" or "society seek only to use creation in order to dominate other men, to gain power for themselves, to enrich themselves at the expense of others, then the 'world' becomes in some sense the victim of their greed and it takes on the character of those who make use of it in a sinful way. It is the 'world' in this sense that the Christian and the monk must liberate himself from." Merton's advice to this youth is succinct: "Make a better world than we have handed on to you" (RJ 347–49).

The theme of making a better world emerges again in Merton's brief correspondence with Erling Thumberg, founder of the International Center for Integrative Studies (ICIS) who invites Merton to be a sponsor for "The Door," a project for youth. To this request to support a youth model for a caring human community, Merton responds that he applauds the center's concern for the dangers of technology, which disrupts the ecological balance of things, and asks to be listed as an "author and poet."[27]

It is clear that Merton's world is indeed larger than the Abbey of Gethsemani or the state of Kentucky or the West. His Working Notebooks for this period indicate the international scope of his reading and thinking: Kenneth Jackson, Kuno Meyer, Mechtilde of Magdeberg, Karl Barth, Ibn al-Arabi, Hugo Rahner, Flannery O'Connor, Hans Urs von Balthasar, Eugène Ionesco, Edwin Muir, Dietrich Bonhoeffer, Josef Pieper, Michel Foucault, Rainer Maria Rilke, Saint Irenaeus of Lyons, Jean-Paul Sartre, Ivan Fyodorov, William Faulkner, Octavio Paz, Susan Sontag, Isaac of Nineveh, Saint Augustine, William Styron, Celtic monasticism, Zen mysticism, Hesychasm, Christian and Buddhist dialogue—to name just a few. Supported by his reading of the Islamic poet-mystic Ibn al-Arabi, who espouses a position that the world "is created anew at every single moment,"[28] and Hugo Rahner's statement that "man is the incarnate dialogue with God,"[29] Merton continues to steep himself in Eastern and Western thinking. After copying this Rahner quote in his notebook, which Merton calls a "beautiful sentence," he adds his own commentary: "But God speaks his word also in *Creation*—hence for all men there is a possibility of dialogue with Him in and through their own being and in their relation to the world in which He has placed them" (Merton's emphasis).

Merton's public stance on ecology gains an even broader audience in February 1968, when he reviews Roderick Nash's first edition of *Wilderness and the American Mind*. Although his Working Notebook 34 includes a list of books on the American frontier and several of John Muir's writings to support his study of Nash's text,[30] Merton's journal entry for February 25 includes an apparently insignificant comment: "Yesterday I wrote a short piece on Wilderness (the Nash book) in the afternoon. Importance of the 'ecological conscience.' (Same war as above!!)" The war reference is obviously to Vietnam, a conflict that continues to frustrate Merton, but—judging from his journal jotting for that day and the previous day—he refers also to American imperialist policies that are "raging an undeclared war against more than a billion people," as well as his own failings as a hermit when "more real solitude" and "moderation" are called for (OSM 58).

Contrary to Merton's casual regard for his essay "The Wild Places," this "short piece" that he apparently dashed off in one sitting comprises a significant statement on his evolving ecological vision (PAJ 95–107). Published during the summer of 1968 in the *Catholic Worker* and the *Center Magazine*, Merton's essay skillfully summarizes our American attitudes toward the wilderness over three and a half centuries and ends with a stirring challenge.[31] He recaps the Puritans' "tradition of repugnance for nature" and their sacred duty to "combat, reduce, destroy, and transform the wilderness"; the nineteenth-century landscape painters' and James Fenimore Cooper's reverence for the "Noble Primitive who grew up in the 'honesty of the woods'"; Thoreau and the Transcendentalists' view of nature as a healing symbol and therefore the necessity to protect an "element of wildness"; John Muir's commitment to preserve wilderness through a federal park system; Theodore Roosevelt's conservation impulse to support hunting and what might be called the "cult of virility"; and Aldo Leopold's principles for ethical land use.

Once again using the book review format as an opportunity to discuss his current interests and beliefs, Merton goes beyond summarizing the text to criticize Nash for remaining in the historical mode and failing to recognize "the tragic implications of this inner contradiction." With a nod to Rachel Carson as another voice that recognizes the "sickness in ourselves," Merton identifies what he regards as the crucial issue facing humankind, namely, that the savagery that the Puritans projected "out there" onto the wilderness is in reality savagery within the human heart. For Merton the Manichean matter-spirit split had collapsed long before. Now he calls on us, the readers, to recognize our own twisted thinking—to identify the ironic ways we continue to honor the wilderness myth while continuing to destroy the wilderness itself. Merton challenges us to come to terms with the deep conflict imposed by our patriarchal and oppressive culture, that is, the tension between the wilderness mystique and the mystique of exploitation and power in the name of freedom and creativity. "Take away the space, the freshness, the rich spontaneity of a wildly flourishing nature," Merton writes,

> and what will become of the creative pioneer mystique? A pioneer in a suburb is a sick man tormenting himself with projects of virile conquest. In a ghetto he is a policeman shooting every black man who gives him a dirty look. Obviously, the frontier is a thing of the past, the bison has vanished, and only by some miracle have a few Indians managed to survive. There are still some forests and wilderness areas, but we are firmly established as an urban culture. Nevertheless, the problem of ecology exists in a most acute form. The danger of fallout and atomic waste is only one of the more spectacular ones. (PAJ 104)

Merton's biting analysis of our contemporary social ills is telling. He regards our racial injustice, our bizarre fascination with war, our commitment to an industrial-technological complex, and our wanton destruction of the planet—with napalm, DDT, and everyday wastefulness—as related. Our adherence to an illusion that we are "in charge" of the cosmos and that we "justify [our] existence and . . . attain bliss (temporal, eternal, or both) by transforming nature into wealth" seduces us into a distorted relationship with humans and with the very nature that sustains us. Merton's opening sentence to "The Wild Places" is a clue to his thesis: "Man is a creature of ambiguity" and our task is "recognizing our self-contradictions." And, indeed, this thirteen-page article is about just that: recognizing our self-contradictions that compel us to make choices of domination that bring "a quick return on somebody's investment—and a permanent disaster for everybody else" (PAJ 105).

Merton concludes his review, as Nash does his book, with a section on Aldo Leopold, who well understood, says Merton, "that the erosion of American land was only part of a more drastic erosion of American freedom" (PAJ 105). Merton applauds Leopold for clearly articulating one of the most "important moral discoveries of our time": an ecological conscience, that is, "an awareness of man's true place as a dependent member of the biotic community" (PAJ 105–6). Awareness! That word again: becoming fully human and awake to our surroundings and then seeing it anew with eyes of compassion and responsibility. The tragedy of our time, Merton continues, is our misplaced reverence toward goods, money, property. We "mistake," he writes, "the artificial value of inert objects and abstractions for the power of life itself. Against this ethic Aldo Leopold laid down a basic principle of the ecological conscience: 'A thing is right when it tends to preserve the integrity, stability, and beauty of the biotic community. It is wrong when it tends otherwise.'" Furthermore, the "very character of the war in Vietnam—with crop poisoning, the defoliation of forest trees, the incineration of villages and their inhabitants with napalm— presents a stark enough example to remind us of this most urgent moral need" (PAJ 106–7). What a telling indictment of many of our current industrial, military, and political practices and what a challenge to transform how we regard all life! Merton summarizes his discussion by reminding us—lest we not make the connection—that an "ecological conscience is also essentially a peace-making conscience." This strong declaration of the interdependence of human and nonhuman creation and our special responsibility for environmental integrity encapsulates Merton's evolving ecological vision—a vision born from multiple seeds of experience and contemplation. In the penultimate paragraph of the essay, Merton poses a piercing question to all of us: "Can Aldo Leopold's ecological conscience become effective in America today?" Merton leaves us to grapple with an answer, and he concludes his book review with a quasi-humorous comment that he is one of those sporting a "Celebrate Life!" button and "bearing witness as best we can to these tidings" (PAJ 107).

Just as Rachel Carson had written a text more timely than she perhaps knew, Merton creates a seminal, even prophetic, piece that becomes his last published statement on the challenges facing contemporary society. Although Merton's journal comment downplays the importance of this book review and metaphorically consigns it to the duties of ordinary time, this is indeed a graced moment in his evolving consciousness, one that brings to a head his commitment to human and ecological justice.

Merton had actually been thinking through these issues and particularly the concept of an ecological conscience for several months. His reading of Nash's book had been percolating in his mind. Two letters to Barbara Hubbard, a dedicated futurist and director of the Center of American Living in New York, in December 1967 and February 1968, attest to his ongoing concern about environmental integrity, and many of his sentiments echo and expand his comments to Rachel Carson nearly five years earlier.[32] In his December 23 letter to Hubbard, Merton offers four points that are a response to her request to offer a religious perspective to two questions: "What do we know about the relationship between Man and the process of organic and cultural evolution that can guide us forward now?" and "What is really New now? Is this or is this not a moment of evolutionary transcendence?"[33] Merton's comments are subsequently published in the Center Letter 3. He notes: (1) humanity is poised on "one of the crucial thresholds of [its] existence"; (2) what is new is that we now have the knowledge and power to affect not just individuals, but life itself—discovering the implications of our actions is crucial; (3) we need to make "life-affirming" decisions, not from our current "thought system that is largely programmed by unconscious death drives, destructiveness, greed, etc."; (4) we need to admit "we are still problems to ourselves. Where the religious dimension enters in is . . . in a radical self-criticism and openness and a profound ability to *trust* not only in our chances of a winning gamble, but in an inner dynamism of life itself, a basic creativity, a power of life to win over entropy and death." His concluding paragraph to Hubbard compliments her efforts to bring together voices from different disciplines: "It shows the realization of one of our greatest needs: a real expansion of communication to its worldwide limits. I wish you success" (WF 72–73; Merton's emphasis).

Two months later, Merton writes to Barbara Hubbard again, responding to her February 12 letter, in which she ponders technology's power to "propel earth-born forces out of the womb of earth" and shares her intent to devise a questionnaire about "the meaning of man's entry into space," a topic Merton admits he does not know well, yet resists because of the "commercialism, hubris, and cliché" surrounding it.[34] Nevertheless, technological innovations and space exploration prompt Merton to remind Hubbard that what we think and do *now* has critical consequences. Hence, Merton outlines what he perceives as two opposing positions: a *millennial consciousness* and an *ecological consciousness*. A millennial consciousness regards the past and present as mere prologue to what is really coming and what is really worth valuing; an ecological consciousness, quite the opposite, is aware (that word again!) of the value of everything in creation. A millennial consciousness is ready to "destroy and repudiate the past" so that "the big event will happen." "This consciousness," writes Merton, "is found in Marxism, in Black Power, in Cargo Cults, in Church aggiornamento, in Third World revolutionary movements." The ecological consciousness, on the other hand, "says: look out!" Be careful about what you discard. "We are not alone in this thing. We belong to a community of living beings and we owe our fellow members in this community the respect and honor due to them. If we are to enter into a new era, well and good, but let's bring the rest of the living along with us. In other words, we must not try to prepare the millennium by immolating our living earth, by careless and stupid exploitation for short-term commercial, military, or technological ends which will be paid for by irreparable loss in living species and natural resources" (WF 74).

Citing Albert Schweitzer and Aldo Leopold as appropriate spokespersons for environmental integrity, Merton reminds Hubbard of Schweitzer's maxim: "Life is sacred . . . that of plants and animals [as well as that of our] fellow man"; he includes, as well, Leopold's "expansion of the Golden Rule" in his definition of an ecological conscience. For Merton the panorama of space exploration offers an opportunity for moral choice. Exploring another geography—spacescape—with a millennial conscience will lead to "ecological irresponsibility." Far preferable would be an "ecological ethic" that involves "deepening of the ecological sense" and a "corresponding restraint and wisdom in the way we treat the earth we live on and the other members of the ecological community with which we live." Merton ends his letter with yet another gesture to the button-sporting generation of the 1960s; he suggests "distributing a new button" that urges "Put Flower Power into Space" (WF 74–75).

Surely, Thomas Merton was ahead of his time in challenging us to adopt Aldo Leopold's concept of an ecological conscience. Truth be told, Leopold's principles for ethical land use eventually became the blueprint for U.S. federal environmental legislation in the 1980s and 1990s. But laws can easily be disregarded and principles forgotten, as we have witnessed all too often in the promulgation and then reversal of environmental policy over the last twenty years. Only those who are awake to the legislative changes and executive orders that negate previous attempts to be responsible stewards of creation realize that we have yet to really heed the warning of *Silent Spring*. DDT, banned in the United States in 1972, is still controversially used for disease control in developing countries. Only those who are awake to the current controversies surrounding oil in the Arctic Wildlife Refuge, reservoirs of natural gas in the New York and Pennsylvania Marcellus Shale, offshore drilling in the Gulf of Mexico, the contest for water rights in America and Africa, depletion of the ozone layer and our rainforests, climate change and the receding polar ice cap, and the quest for renewable energy and clean water realize how prophetic Thomas Merton's final writings are.

I have written elsewhere that, had Merton lived beyond December 10, 1968, he would have been in the vanguard of contemporary nature

The Wilderness Society

729 FIFTEENTH STREET, N.W., WASHINGTON, D. C. 20005

MEMBERSHIP CERTIFICATE

*THIS IS TO CERTIFY THAT*

- Thomas Merton
  Abbey of Gethsemani
  Trappist, Kentucky  40073

is a __Contributing__ member of the Society

until __May 1969__   *Harvey Broome*
                      President

PURPOSE AND AIM

To secure the preservation of wilderness...to carry on an educational program concerning the value of wilderness and how it may best be used and preserved in the public interest...to make and encourage scientific studies concerning wilderness... and to mobilize cooperation in resisting the invasion of wilderness.

Front and back sides of Merton's membership card for the Wilderness Society.

writers and environmentalists "not simply because creation is holy, but because we humans have a moral obligation to be the voice for the voiceless."[35] It is no simple coincidence that when Merton's body was flown from Bangkok to the monastery at Gethsemani, his membership card in the Wilderness Society (Aldo Leopold being one of the 1935 cofounders) was discovered among his belongings. Before leaving for Asia, Merton had written on the inside cover of Working Notebook

36, "Where are we really going? Always home," along with a list of places he wanted to see in Asia. On August 22 he had written, in capital letters spaced out on the notebook page, an adage from his long-time literary hero, William Blake: "Cleanse the doors of perception."[36] It would seem that Merton's lifelong commitment to becoming more awake, to seeing the holy in the ordinary, and to realizing the contemplative energy of outer and inner landscapes had indeed cleansed his perception. In his last years Merton was discovering that peace and justice are intimately connected and that, because we are all linked through a web of biological and spiritual relationships, nature—that is, all creation—is entitled to justice. As Belden Lane has commented: "Merton's call for social justice in the 1960s was no faddish participation in the restive activism of the decade, but a natural consequence of his commitment to contemplation. He knew, for example, that disciplined and creative nonviolent action is only possible for those who have begun a journey into emptiness."[37]

Had Merton lived beyond December 1968, he probably would have written a series of cutting-edge essays on ecojustice to complement his profound and visionary statements on social justice. If, as he asserts in his review of Roderick Nash's book, an ecological conscience is "essentially a peace-making conscience," then Merton's commitment to integrating contemplation and action would have come to full flowering in a seminal statement on environmental integrity and our human responsibility for preserving it. In reality, we have many seeds of that unwritten document in Merton's notebooks and journals, his letters to Barbara Hubbard, and his last published book review, of Roderick Nash's text. And those seeds have sprouted in many social gardens.

As an outgrowth of the activism of the 1960s, there are now literally hundreds of organizations devoted to environmental responsibility and ecological awareness at the local, regional, national, and international levels—Greenpeace, the Wilderness Society, the Sierra Club, and World Wildlife Fund being perhaps the most widely recognized. To their credit, the major religions have enlarged their theology of justice to include environmental justice. Though the dharma has traditionally taught that all things are connected, the International Network of Engaged Buddhists today more consciously calls its followers to practice the principle of interdependence; proponents of Hinduism are publishing tracts and books articulating the ramifications of the intersection of Earth, sky, and water, and the Coalition on the Environment and Jewish Life offers a speaker's bureau on Judaism and ecology. As early as the 1970s the World Council of Churches began writing about our human responsibility for the welfare of creation and in 1983 designed a process called "Justice, Peace, and Creation" that expanded in 1988 to the Ecumenical Earth Program, which respects "the diverse unity of the whole inhabited earth." In January of that same year, the bishops of the Philippines issued a statement challenging their people to "develop a deep appreciation for the fragility of our islands, life-systems and take steps to defend the Earth. It is a matter of life and death." Currently, in Manila every third Sunday is dedicated to prayer and reflection on ecology. The *Catechism of the Catholic Church* expands the traditional Christian understanding of the seventh commandment ("Thou shalt not steal") to include responsibility to respect the integrity of creation. In recent years Popes John Paul II and Benedict XVI have written encyclicals on the environment (*Centesimus Annus, Caritas in Veritate*) and dedicated their January 1 World Day of Peace address to explicitly link peace with all our human and nonhuman brothers and sisters. As recently as January 2010, Pope Benedict XVI's New Year message counseled: "If you want to cultivate peace, protect creation."[38]

Merton's position on our responsibility for human and ecojustice is not merely a mid-twentieth-century scholarly curiosity. Too many streams of scientific and religious thought have converged in the last fifty years that demonstrate the wisdom of his prophetic vision. Any number of contemporary scientific and spiritual writers—such as Wernher von Braun, John Polkinghorne, Arno Penzias, Paul Davies, Chet Raymo, Stephen Hawking, Brian Swimme, Thomas Berry, Diarmuid O'Murchu, Leonardo Boff, Denis Edwards, Elizabeth Johnson, Sean McDonagh, Judy Cannato, and Sallie McFague—have in recent years written convincingly about the new cosmology, our planetary interdependence, and our responsibility to make decisions based on the long-term health of the Earth community of which we are a part. Our job is to become awake, to read, and to act. In the challenging words of the poet Mary Oliver, "Tell me, what is it you plan to do / With your one wild and precious life?"[39]

If, as Thomas Merton says, an "ecological conscience is also essentially a peace-making conscience," then surely the gauntlet has been tossed down. The life of the planet is experiencing its most intense crisis. Our "one wild and precious life" is at stake. The challenge to develop an ecological conscience has been issued. All creation, human and nonhuman, awaits our response. It's all about becoming awake, expanding our vision, and learning to act responsibly. In Merton's words to Rachel Carson: "the duty of our age, the 'vocation' of modern man is to unite them [technics and wisdom] in a supreme humility which will result in a totally self-forgetful creativity and service. Can we do this?" (WF 71).

Indeed, can we do this?

*Afterword*

# Woodland Deer
## An Ecological Journey in Miniature

> The deer reveals to me something essential in myself.
> —Thomas Merton, *Dancing in the Waters of Life*

I hesitate to say more about the influence of nature on Thomas Merton's spirituality, but there is one creature that singularly intrigued Merton in his weeks and months at the hermitage: deer. In fact, if we examine closely his frequent interaction with this mysterious woodland creature, we can notice that the changes in Merton's attitude to them—from mere curiosity to compassion and a feeling of responsibility for their well-being—mirror the trajectory of his monastic life and his increasing sense of responsibility for environmental integrity.

By my count, there are twenty-two references to deer in Merton's journals between 1963 and 1968—everything from a rumor that there might be deer in the woods to a humorous report from Andy Boone, the monastery's eccentric neighbor, that deer are raping his cows. The theologian and literary critic George Kilcourse has written with insight about Merton's use of deer imagery in his "poetry of the forest," linking this graceful, mysterious creature to Merton's concept of the True Self, and Robert Waldron has highlighted Merton's frequent references to deer as a "moment of true contemplative prayer," which signals how deeply Merton's ability to see is maturing.[1] I would, however, like to suggest a different approach. Embedded in this collection of deer references is a sequence of thirteen consecutive passages between

January 1965 and June 1966 that creates a symphony of meaning worthy of examination. Indeed, this sequence of deer references reveals in miniature the larger spiritual transformation in Merton's life. Emulating Merton's fondness for metaphor and analogy, I use the word *symphony* deliberately: his transformative interaction with deer follows the musical structure of the first movement of a symphony: exposition, development, and recapitulation or coda.

## Exposition: Fascination and Intimacy

The exposition of the beginning of a symphony, in proper classical style, may include both dramatic and lyrical themes. Merton's response to the presence of deer in the area surrounding his hermitage is both. For example, after an emotionally charged feast of Epiphany in January 1965, Merton "suddenly realized that there were beings there—deer . . . at least five. They stood still looking at me, and I stood looking at them, a lovely moment that stretched into ten minutes perhaps!" (DWL 189). Merton is captivated by the drama of the moment, a subtle, almost imperceptible realization that he is in the presence of the Holy. Nine months later, his second interaction with deer introduces a lyrical theme. Merton has moved to the hermitage full-time a few days before, and so his chance of seeing deer in the woods increases. His fascination begins with an "intellectual" approach, studying two stags and two does through field glasses, but that fascination quickly develops into a lyrical, inward reverie. Captivated by "their beautiful running, grazing," Merton regards everything about them as "completely lovely." Like the prehistoric cave painters, Merton is also *seeing into* the deer, awakening to the *haecceitas* or *thisness* of the creature, which Gerard Manley Hopkins called inscape. "It is an awe-inspiring thing—the *Mantu* or 'spirit' shown in the running of the deer, the 'deerness' that sums up everything and is sacred and marvelous. A contemplative intuition! Yet perfectly ordinary, everyday seeing. The deer reveals to me something essential in myself! . . . I could sense the softness of their coat and longed to touch them" (DWL 291). This

A solitary deer on the front lawn of the hermitage. (Photo by Harry L. Hinkle; courtesy of the photographer)

September encounter with the deer is a deep and powerful moment for Merton; he is not only appreciating the graceful woodland creatures in the external world, but reflecting on the universal spiritual significance of the animal. He is moving from a solely outward, scientific glance at the exterior landscape to an inward glance at the spiritual meaning of creation and the geography of his own heart. He recognizes his link with his human ancestors, as well as the divine spark he and the deer share with Being itself.

This deeply satisfying moment of fellowship is not as rare as it may seem. Native peoples often speak of the human and animal worlds as "parallel cultures" on two sides of a chasm, occasionally crossed by the shaman to make inquiries. Gretel Ehrlich explains the influence of nature on us this way. When we discover a certain interdependence with animals, we encounter "intimacy with what is animal in me." The animal and I are "comrades who save each other's lives." We form an odd partnership, "stripped-down compassion, one that is made of frankness and respect and rigorously excludes sentimentality."[2]

This same unspoken intimacy underpins Merton's journal comments four days later, when he describes how a doe has become so used to him that she does not move while he is pacing back and forth in front of the hermitage saying Compline. To his delight, the deer "even came down the field *towards me!*" (DWL 292; Merton's emphasis). This new tameness is cause for both elation and alarm as Merton remembers the impending hunting season. Once again Ehrlich's words offer insight into the meaning of this sense of intimacy and the effect of nature on our deepest identity. "An animal's wordlessness takes on the cleansing qualities of space: . . . what is obvious to an animal is . . . what's bedrock and current in us: aggression, fear, insecurity, happiness, or equanimity. Because they have the ability to read our involuntary tics and scents, we're transparent to them and thus exposed—we're finally ourselves."[3] Merton would agree with Ehrlich's insight, for he comments later in that journal entry how sane and authentic he feels in this new solitude of the ordinary: "quiet supper, reading, walking, looking at the hills, the silence, the moon, the does, darkness, prayer, bed" (DWL 293). This lyricism continues to play out on the feast of Saint Francis of Assisi, October 4, when Merton declares a holiday and "walked through the hollow then to the long field and in and out the wood where the deer sleep" (DWL 300).

## Development: Communion and Compassion

The next several deer passages in Merton's journal reveal increased tempo, dramatic tension, competing forces; Merton is at his literary best. During October and November 1965 Merton has been reading Heidegger and Isaac of Stella on the themes of ontology and nothingness. He has also been reflecting on the excesses and arrogant tone of his own writing, believing he is writing too much and not knowing how to say "no." His next paragraph, however, like the comet he has been seeking in the night sky for several evenings, streaks off in a blaze of exultation.

Using the introductory word *Riches*, Merton begins his account with quasi field notes about the comet and the reflection of its tail. Moving into metaphor, he praises the beauty and emotional effect of "this great spear in the sky." Illustrating with poetic dexterity the context of this cosmic phenomenon, Merton describes how acorns drop around him, the monastery bell signals the most sacred moment of Roman Catholic Mass, meteorites flash across the sky, military planes invade the space, and the stag cries out beyond his hedge. Closing the passage with a repetition of the word *Riches*, Merton then joyfully recites Psalm 18. Here, the outer world of natural landscape becomes a landscape of the sacred, flowering into a prayer of praise. The psalm proclaims the "heavens are telling the glory of God and the firmament proclaims his handiwork"—a world in which the voice of all creation is heard, in which humans and nature are in right relationship with one another and with God, "my rock and redeemer" (DWL 312–13).

In one short paragraph Merton moves from scientific observation to picturesque composition of scene. He creates contrasts between the comet in deep space and the intrusion of the Strategic Air Command plane, symbol of all that is wrong with the American military-industrial complex. Note that the deer is not central to this passage. Is its cry a coincidence of timing? Mere poetic addition? Or a subtle commentary on the disharmony brought about by military buildup, the nuclear arms race, and war itself? Whatever the motive, the intensity of the moment, underscored by the repeated word *Riches*, catapults Merton into a psalm of exultation.

Caught up in the awesome experience of this cosmic phenomenon, Merton is something of a psalmist himself, using several rhetorical strategies to describe the experience: poetic contrast between nature in its most mysterious manifestation and its interruption by human implements of destruction; the numerical sequence of three meteorites, two planes, and one deer; and the carefully chosen *epanalepsis*, *Riches*, to bookend the passage. From captivation to scientific study to personal insight and intimacy, Merton has advanced to a new level of communion, even ecstasy, that lays the groundwork for an even deeper encounter with Mystery itself—one that evokes compassion.

Midmorning a week later, Merton spots a wounded deer limping in the field, "one leg incapacitated." Caught up with the sacredness of all creations in his world, Merton is overwhelmed with compassion, finding himself "weeping bitterly" at the sight; yet the deer, after giving him a long look, "bounded off without any sign of trouble" (DWL 315–16). Once again parallel cultures have reached across the chasm for some kind of deep, inexplicable communication. Merton never alludes to a mistaken impression or a miracle. He merely sketches the scene in bare detail and surrounds it with mystery, anticipating and validating Annie Dillard's dictum that the natural world is embedded in mystery, and "the extravagant gesture is the very stuff of creation."[4] The impulse of compassion is evident again less than a month later, when Merton lists among five points of environmental destruction a statement that two deer have been found dead nearby "not shot, but just dead. Poisoned by chemicals?" (DWL 323).

At first glance this comment may seem perfunctory or anticlimactic after the drama of the comet and Merton's soaring language. From another perspective, his concern for the dead deer indicates the degree to which his vision has broadened. As Isaiah 32:16 reminds us, "It is in the wildness that justice comes to live." Deer are no longer the Other, to be viewed through field glasses, but fellow inhabitants of the woods worthy of compassion and protection. Having been enticed to study the deer, in a process the ethnobotanist Gary Nabhan dubs "hot flashes," Merton has allowed these encounters with deer to influence his inner life, often experiencing communion with them in their mutual silence and solitude. Now compassion prompts a minimal level of responsibility for them.

## Recapitulation and Coda: Responsibility

Recapitulation in a movement of a symphony allows the composer to return to all the themes already introduced, play with variations of them, and conclude with a final statement. Merton's interaction with deer follows this same pattern. In January and February 1966 Merton notes the morning tracks of a small deer and two deer that bounded away in "long slow curving leaps" (LL 18). In March, after the worst of the winter has passed, Merton and the deer are again studying each other (LL 25). These passages represent a reprise of all the motifs of the previous autumn: field glasses, five deer, a snapshot description of their movement, and again the fascination. But in May and June Merton writes about the deer with two variations or modifications, the first a poetic image celebrating intimacy and communion, the second a vignette of an actual experience with deer that functions as a parable of responsibility.

Inserted into his journal for May 7, 1966, is a love poem for "M," the nurse Merton had met and fallen in love with after back surgery in March (LL 52–53). The poem recalls their meeting that day, Derby Day, finding quiet time together against the backdrop of the private jets landing for the ceremonies at Churchill Downs. The poem also re-creates a literary Eden for the lovers into which "love walks gently as a deer / to where we sit on the green grass." This is no physical deer but the universal, symbolic deer—what Merton calls the Mantu, or inner spirit—of generations past, together with allusions to Genesis and the Song of Songs—in all its intense yet gentle mystery, an apt image of Merton's relationship with "M." Merton's ability to be awake, aware of immediate reality, inspires metaphor to express the ineffable—not the ineffable experience of agape, the mysterious love of God for humans, but eros, the equally mysterious and valued love between human beings. Not surprisingly, deer, so wild, untamable, and exotic to our human ways of thinking, is clearly linked with Merton's wild, untamable, and exotic love for "M."

The second variation of these restated themes is Merton's action on behalf of his much-loved woodland creatures. In June 1966 he shoots "be-bes" at some dogs that have been hectoring the doe in his woods—not to kill them, but to "sting them good" and, he hopes, deter their aggressive behavior (LL 331). This act of protection of wildlife has value on the literal level—saving the deer—but also carries symbolic meaning because of its strategic location in volume 6 of his journals, embedded in "A Mid-summer Diary for M," within a passage dated June 22. There Merton has been philosophizing about how he might continue a relationship with "M" in a "deep and lasting, very fruitful form as long as it is part of my solitude." Suddenly the text switches to this vignette of the distressed doe and the annoying dogs. Is this merely a tangential story—variation on a theme—inserted into this text concerning "M" to relieve the heavy tension of deciding what to do about their relationship? Or is it a parable meant to suggest that their love—gentle as a deer—must be protected from badgering outsiders? Is it intended to mean that their love must remain wild and free and that they—Merton and "M"—must be satisfied not with erotic consummation of their love, but with the mysterious union of each other's authentic identity? Or is this perhaps a prophetic and didactic vignette indicating that Merton is at yet another starting point for human decision making? Perhaps this last interpretation is most accurate, for by the end of "A Mid-summer Diary," Merton resolves his struggle over their love by acknowledging that "love and solitude must test each other in the man who means to live alone. . . . I cannot have enough of the hours of silence when nothing happens. When the clouds go by. When the trees say nothing. When the birds sing" (LL 315, 341).

Merton's "A Mid-summer Diary for M" moves quickly to a coda, or closing statement, in which he refers to himself as a deer as well as other wild beings of the woods: "You are in love with a fox, or a deer, or a squirrel. Freedom, darling. That is what the woods mean to me. I am free, free, a wild being, and that is all that I ever can really be. . . . Darling, I am telling you: this life in the woods is IT. It is the only way. . . . All I say is that it is the life that has chosen itself for me" (LL 342). Merton's decision to "marry the silence of the forest," as he wrote a year earlier in *Day of a Stranger,* is irrevocable. Like Thoreau, Merton is committed to the "tonic of wildness."[5]

If we look at these thirteen deer passages as representing one cycle of seasons, Merton has come a long way from mere fascination with these graceful woodland creatures. The deer evoke in Merton spiritual insight and move him to action. Indeed, they become a kind of icon of the immanence of God and the movement of grace. Like the deer in the woods, grace can come suddenly as a flash of spiritual insight (spots of time) or gradually as a deeply felt realization (ordinary time). Though the deer are always in the woods—and grace is always available to the soul—silence and solitude are prerequisites for the gift of deeper intimacy. The key, Merton teaches us, is being awake to our physical surroundings and their effect on the geography of our heart. Merton has learned in the depths of his contemplative experience what Rosemary Radford Ruether argues almost twenty-five years later, namely, "the whole ecological community . . . supports and makes possible our existence."[6] If we are to be "seized" by Jesus, if the Incarnation is to be an ongoing grace and not just a historical event, then the Divine must be accessible in the "raw, brute physicality" of this world. If Christ is present in everything—"in Him all things hold together" (Colossians 1:17)—we are all linked as earthy and earthly, interdependent members of his body, responsible to and for one another.

Just as Mozart's *Requiem* was left to the student Franz Süssmayr to finish, so the "unfinished symphony" of Thomas Merton's life looks to us. With environmental crises on multiple fronts, our planet cannot tolerate a "guilty bystander." Merton's life bears witness to our challenge: we need to become more awake, learn to really look at the geography around us, reflect on how it contributes to our identity, and discover how we, through contemplation, are called to maintain its integrity. We need to examine the landscape of our own hearts, encouraging impulses of compassion for those humans and nonhumans who need our care and protection. We need to heed the invitation of spiritual writers and scientists to explore the new cosmology in order to expand our horizons and discover our simultaneous dependence on God and on each being in our universe. And we need to use the advances in technology, with their "immense potential for facilitating unity," not as "cultural idols of greed and domination" but as gifts "in the service of the whole of life."[7] In short, we need to develop an ecological conscience.

# Notes

## Introduction

1. Worster, *Nature's Economy*, 2nd ed., ix–x.
2. Merton, *Cold War Letters*.
3. Wordsworth, *The Prelude*.
4. Heinrich, *Ravens in Winter;* see also his *Mind of the Raven*.
5. Nelson, *Make Prayers to the Raven*, 248; quoted in Wheat, "Metamorphosis in Myth," 17.

## 1. Encountering Rachel Carson

1. Watson, "Sounding the Alarm." See also Linda J. Lear, "Rachel Carson's *Silent Spring*."
2. Lear, *Rachel Carson*, 118–19. Lear makes the point that this rejection by *Reader's Digest* was fortunate because when Carson returned to the subject of pesticides in the 1960s, she did so not as a federal employee but as a private citizen.
3. Lear, introduction to Carson, *Silent Spring*, 2002, xi.
4. Watson, "Sounding the Alarm," 116; Lear, *Rachel Carson*, 428–40.
5. Gore, introduction to Carson, *Silent Spring*, 1994, xv.
6. Lear, *Rachel Carson*, quoted in Watson, "Sounding the Alarm," 115.
7. Lear, introduction to *Silent Spring*, 2002, xii, xiii.
8. Gore, introduction to *Silent Spring*, 1994, xv.
9. Lyon, *This Incomparable Land*, 13; Gore, introduction to *Silent Spring*, 1994, xv.
10. Conway, *American Literacy*, 243; see also Lyon, *This Incomparable Land*, 13; Gore, introduction to *Silent Spring*, 1994.
11. Kroll, "Ecology as a Subversive Subject," 10–12.

12. Merton's letter is reprinted in *Thomas Merton: A Life in Letters,* 207–10.

13. Merton had already published "Nuclear War and Christian Responsibility" in *Commonweal,* February 9, 1962; "We Have to Make Ourselves Heard" in *Catholic Worker,* May–June 1962; "Peace: A Religious Responsibility," the introduction to *Breakthrough to Peace* (New York: New Directions, 1962); *Original Child Bomb* (New York: New Directions, 1962). He was also periodically disseminating a collection of his Cold War letters in 1961 and 1962. See Burton, *Merton: Vade Mecum,* for a complete listing of letters, poetry, and publications.

14. See Burton, *Merton: Vade Mecum.*

15. Merton, "The Root of War," *Catholic Worker* (October 1961); "The Root of War Is Fear," in *New Seeds of Contemplation* (New York: New Directions, 1961); reprinted in Merton, *Passion for Peace,* 11–19.

16. Kingsolver, *Small Wonder.*

17. Christianity historically has taught the doctrines of incarnation and redemption, sometimes favoring redemption as the great act of Jesus while overlooking the self-emptying love of the Godhead to take on the limitations of human flesh. Creation spirituality and the new cosmology, in conjunction with ecotheologians and ecofeminists, have begun altering this imbalance to focus on the relationship between and among human and nonhuman coinhabitants of this planet.

18. Carson quoted by Lear, introduction to *Silent Spring,* 2002, xix.

19. Nhat Hanh, *Peace Is Every Step.* Merton's belief in nonviolence can be traced to his early awareness of Gandhi when Merton was a student at Oakham and reaches new fulfillment with the publication of *Gandhi on Non-Violence.*

20. Carson's earlier full-length publications *Under the Sea-Wind* (New York: Simon and Schuster, 1941) and *The Sea around Us* (New York: Oxford University Press, 1951) not only made her famous, but enabled her to retire from government service to write full-time.

21. Bate, *The Song of the Earth,* 149.

22. Ibid., 76.

23. Lyon, *This Incomparable Land,* 99.

## 2. Learning to See

1. *Messiah* by George Frideric Handel was originally performed in Dublin on April 13, 1742, during the Easter season. When it was brought to colonial America, performances were scheduled during the Christmas season, which inaugurated the tradition of performances being held at that time.

2. Emerson, "Nature," 24.

3. Keats, "Letter to George and Thomas Keats," *Selected Poems and Letters*, 260–61; see also "Letter to Richard Woodhouse," ibid., 279–80.

4. Thoreau, *Walden*, 264.

5. Burroughs, "The Art of Seeing Things," in *Leaf and Tendril*, 1–25; reprinted in McKibben, *American Earth*, 146–59.

6. Lane, *The Solace of Fierce Landscapes*, 187.

7. Julian of Norwich, *Revelations of Divine Love*. Thomas Aquinas is quoted in Matthew Fox, *The Coming of the Cosmic Christ*, 115.

8. O'Collins and Farrugia, *A Concise Dictionary of Theology*, 231.

9. Weil, *Waiting for God*, xxxi.

10. Hieb, *Inner Journeying through Art-Journaling*, 59, 87.

11. Nepo, *The Book of Awakening*, 54–55.

12. Blake, "The Marriage of Heaven and Hell," 39.

13. Merton, *No Man Is an Island*, 33.

14. Burroughs, "The Art of Seeing Things," in McKibben, *American Earth*, 151–52.

15. Nepo, *The Book of Awakening*, 54.

16. Hieb, *Inner Journeying through Art-Journaling*, 88, 33.

17. Waldron, *Thomas Merton: Master of Attention*, 25; Hieb refers to this commitment to transformation as a "contract with delight" in *Inner Journeying through Art-Journaling*, 87.

18. Lopez, "A Literature of Place," 23–25.

19. Hieb, *Inner Journeying through Art-Journaling*, 22.

20. Ruth Merton, *Tom's Book*, n.p. All quotations referring to this early period of Merton's life are from this handset, unpaginated, and limited edition of Ruth Jenkins Merton's account of her son's early years.

21. Lopez, "A Literature of Place," 24.

22. In June 2002 the principal of the Collège Ingres presented Donald Grayston with a photocopy of the program for the annual scholastic awards. At the end of the 1926–1927 academic year, Thomas Merton received recognition on the Tableau D'Honneur (honor roll) as well as prizes for English, gymnastics (first prize in his age group) and *escrime* (fencing). At the end of the 1927–1928 academic year, Merton received recognition on the Tableau de Satisfaction (a lower ranking than the previous year) and prizes for French language, history/geography, and *dessin artistique et modelage* (drawing and modeling).

23. Lopez, "A Literature of Place," 25.

24. Wordsworth, *The Prelude*, book 5, line 382.

25. Blake, "The Marriage of Heaven and Hell," 34–35.

26. Moffitt, "To Look at Any Thing," 21.

27. Shannon, Bochen, and O'Connell, *The Thomas Merton Encyclopedia*, 319.

## 3. "Spots of Time"

1. Weis, "Beyond the Shadow and the Disguise." Both Merton and Wordsworth were orphaned at an early age, sent away to school, proved to be unruly in their adolescent years, and had to be reined in by guardians because of financial and sexual excesses.

2. Merton, "The Art of Poetry," Columbia University class notes (1938), n.p. Quoted in Mott, *The Seven Mountains of Thomas Merton*, 110.

3. Wordsworth, *The Prelude*. All poem references are to the 1850 version in the edition edited by Wordsworth, Abrams, and Gill.

4. Ibid., book 5, line 382.

5. Hopkins, "The Windhover: To Christ Our Lord," in *The Poems of Gerard Manley Hopkins*, 69.

6. Merton, *Witness to Freedom*, 277–78. See also Merton to Louis Massignon, July 20, 1960, in *Thomas Merton: A Life in Letters*, 356–57.

7. I am indebted to William H. Shannon for this insight.

## 4. Seeing Differently

1. Rilke, *Rilke's Book of Hours*, 14.

2. Greeley, *The Catholic Imagination*, 1.

3. Merton, *Bread in the Wilderness*, 3.

4. Eliade, *Patterns in Comparative Religion*, 369.

5. Merton, *Day of a Stranger*. Written in May 1965, this text was first published in a South American journal, later in the *Hudson Review* 20 (1967), and posthumously in book form in 1981.

6. Greeley, *The Catholic Imagination*, 46.

7. See Susan Vreeland's historical novel of the painter Emily Carr, *The Forest Lover*.

8. William Blake, "Auguries of Innocence," 481–84, lines 1–2.

9. Szabo, introduction to Merton, *In the Dark before Dawn*, xxii.

10. Ibid., xxi.

11. Francis X. Connolly, one of the founders of the Catholic Poetry Society of America and associate editor of its magazine, *Spirit*, was acquainted with Merton's youthful poetry during the 1940s and early 1950s; in his November 1946 review of *A Man in the Divided Sea*, Connolly updated his readers on Merton's entrance into the Trappist monastery at Gethsemani as "not a flight from life but a perfectly natural step forward." It was Connolly who later advised Merton to include in the final pages of *The Seven Storey Mountain* his commentary on the contemplative life, previously published in *Commonweal*; in an editorial on *The Seven Storey Mountain* in the March 1949 issue of *Thought*, Connolly presents

Merton as a "prize-winning poet" with three volumes of poetry already to his credit. See my article "Merton's Poetry: Early Recognition."

12. Norris, preface to Merton, *In the Dark before Dawn,* xv.

13. Merton, *In the Dark before Dawn,* xxiii.

14. O'Hara, "'The Whole World . . . Has Appeared as a Transparent Manifestation of the Love of God,'" 107.

15. O'Donohue, "The Inner History of a Day," 161.

16. Lane, *The Solace of Fierce Landscapes,* 37–50.

17. Williams, *Red: Passion and Patience in the Desert,* 144.

18. In 1964 Merton was reading several books by Kenneth H. Jackson and others on early Celtic poetry (*Studies in Early Celtic Nature Poetry,* 1935, and *A Celtic Miscellany,* 1951). His notes on page 27 of Working Notebook 14 connect the birdsong calendars mentioned by Jackson with the calendar of Pseudo Bede from the Durham manuscript MS PL *Patrologia Latina* Migne 90:761.

19. Labrie, *Thomas Merton and the Inclusive Imagination,* 244.

20. Earlier that year, on January 21, 1963, Merton writes: "Sunrise calls forth solemn music from the depths of my being: disposition of order in my whole day."

21. Lane, *Landscapes of the Sacred,* 46, 103.

22. Ehrlich, *The Solace of Open Spaces,* 5.

23. Lane, *Landscapes of the Sacred,* 103.

24. St. John, "Deep Geography," 52.

25. Ibid., 39–58.

26. Lane, *The Solace of Fierce Landscapes,* 117.

27. Ibid., 170.

28. St. John, "Deep Geography," 39.

29. Lane, *The Solace of Fierce Landscapes,* 225.

30. Austin, *The Land of Little Rain,* 93.

31. Ibid., 94.

32. Abbot Anthony of Egypt, quoted in Lane, *The Solace of Fierce Landscapes,* 165.

33. Shannon, Bochen, and O'Connell, *The Thomas Merton Encyclopedia,* 300–303.

34. Bate, *The Song of the Earth,* 109.

35. Byron, "Darkness," in *The Poetical Works of Byron,* 189–90.

36. Keats, "To Autumn," in *Selected Poems and Letters,* 247–48.

## 5. Merging Inner and Outer Landscapes

1. Grayston, *Thomas Merton's Rewritings* and *Thomas Merton: The Development of a Spiritual Theologian.* See also William H. Shannon, *Something of a Rebel,* 156–59.

2. Grayston, *Thomas Merton's Rewritings*, xx.

3. Ibid., xxxii–xxxiii.

4. Allchin, "The Worship of the Whole Creation," 193.

5. Greeley, *The Catholic Imagination*, 176.

6. Hopkins, "God's Grandeur," in *The Poetry of Gerard Manley Hopkins*, 31.

7. McFague, *The Body of God*, vii.

8. Dillard, *Pilgrim at Tinker Creek*, 77.

9. O'Hara, " 'The Whole World . . . Has Appeared as a Transparent Manifestation of the Love of God,' " 97.

10. Merton, Working Notebook 15, 65; see also the revised version of this reflection in *Cables to the Ace,* in *Collected Poems,* 400.

11. Panikkar, *Blessed Simplicity,* 14; see all of part 1, "The Archetype of the Monk," for a fuller description of his distinction between monk as paradigm (not to be emulated) and monkhood as being one way of discovering our mystical vitality and being more fully human.

12. Ibid., 39.

13. Ibid., 51.

14. Griffin, *Woman and Nature*, 226.

15. Burroughs, "The Art of Seeing Things," reprinted in McKibben, *American Earth,* 147.

16. Merton, *The Hidden Ground of Love,* 158.

17. Bate, *The Song of the Earth,* 263–65.

18. Cunningham, "Thomas Merton: Firewatcher."

19. St. John, "Deep Geography," 56.

20. Mott, *The Seven Mountains of Thomas Merton,* 267.

21. Lentfoehr, *Words and Silence,* 48.

22. Hopkins, "The Blessed Virgin Compared to the Air We Breathe" and "As Kingfishers Catch Fire," in *The Poetry of Gerard Manley Hopkins,* 57, 93.

23. For a keen and comprehensive study of Merton's drawing and calligraphy, see Lipsey, *Angelic Mistakes.*

24. Griffin, *A Hidden Wholeness,* 49.

25. Ibid., 3–4.

26. Ibid., 50.

27. Ibid., 91.

28. Pearson, foreword to Lipsey, *Angelic Mistakes,* xvii.

29. Labrie, *Thomas Merton and the Inclusive Imagination,* 164.

30. Steindl-Rast, "Recollections of Thomas Merton's Last Days in the West," 2.

31. Pearson, "The Ox Mountain Parable," 17.

32. Ibid. Pearson is quoting from *Conjectures of a Guilty Bystander,* 132.

33. Pearson, "The Ox Mountain Parable," 18.

34. O'Hara, "'The Whole World . . . Has Appeared as a Transparent Manifestation of the Love of God,'" 96.

35. Jeffers, "Letter to Sister Mary James Power" (October 1, 1934), 189.

36. Berry, *The Dream of the Earth,* 44.

37. Bernard of Clairvaux, *The Letters of St. Bernard of Clairvaux,* Epistle 106.

## 6. Merton's Evolving Ecological Consciousness

1. Lane, *The Solace of Fierce Landscapes,* 75.

2. See Shannon et al., *The Thomas Merton Encyclopedia,* s.v. "*No Man Is an Island,*" 327–28. Shannon notes that this text is directed primarily at monks and was regarded by Merton as a "sequel" to *Seeds of Contemplation.*

3. Muir, *My First Summer in the Sierra,* 157.

4. See Merton's unpublished notebooks 10–43, at the Thomas Merton Center at Bellarmine University in Louisville.

5. Merton, *Thomas Merton: A Life in Letters.*

6. See Merton, *Cold War Letters.*

7. Kramer, introduction to Merton, *Turning toward the World,* xvi–xvii, xviii, xix.

8. Leopold, *A Sand County Almanac,* 224–25.

9. Prevallet, *In the Service of Life,* 24; emphasis added.

10. Johnson, *Passions for Nature,* 178.

11. Merton, "The Universe as Epiphany," in *Love and Living,* 174–75.

12. Merton, "Teilhard's Gamble," in *Love and Living,* 190. Despite the theological controversy over Teilhard's view of salvation history as embracing not just humans but all creation, it should not surprise modern readers that before the end of the 1960s Joseph Ratzinger acknowledged the value of Teilhard's contribution to Christian thought. In his *Introduction to Christianity* (New York: Herder and Herder, 1969), Ratzinger notes that greater sensitivity to the "cosmic and metaphysical" dimension of Christianity within Eastern Christianity is echoed by Teilhard in his optimistic reading of nature. More recently, as Pope Benedict XVI, Ratzinger has again alluded to the cosmic vision of Teilhard as an explication of Paul's letter to the Romans in which he speaks eloquently of all of creation in labor toward a new birth (Romans 8:19–23). As quoted in the *National*

*Catholic Reporter* by John L. Allen Jr. (July 28, 2009), Pope Benedict said the whole world will one day become an act of worship, a "living host."

13. Plant, "Toward a New World," 1.

14. Hart, *Thomas Merton: First and Last Memories,* n.p.

15. Merton, Working Notebook 11 (1963), 26–27.

16. Macy, advertisement for "The Work That Reconnects" workshop, www.joannamacy.net/theworkthatreconnects.html

17. Millar, lecture, Rochester, N.Y., April 20, 2009; Millar is the current director of the Iona Community, Iona, Scotland.

18. John Macquarrie, *Paths in Spirituality,* 7.

19. Jackson, *Studies in Early Celtic Nature Poetry,* 103.

20. Merton, Working Notebook 14 (June 1964), n.p. (only part of this notebook is paginated). Merton is also taking notes on Kenneth H. Jackson's *A Celtic Miscellany* (London, 1951) and Kuno Meyer's *Selections from Ancient Irish Poetry* (London, 1928).

21. On this point, see Elder, *Reading the Mountains of Home,* 21.

22. Merton, Red Diary 10, n.p. Though this notebook is dated 1959, scholars believe most of the notes were begun after November 1964 and abandoned in early 1965, after Merton's fiftieth birthday.

23. Merton, Notebook 17: "Personal Notes 1965 End–1966 Beginning," n.p. Most of this notebook has been published in Merton, *Dancing in the Water of Life,* 333–49.

24. Thomas Merton's side of the correspondence (1965–1967) is published in *Witness to Freedom,* 312–19; both sides of the correspondence are published in Lord Northbourne, *Religion in the Modern World,* 2nd revised edition.

25. Merton to Gary Snyder, September 20, 1966, Snyder to Merton, October 10, 1966, at the Thomas Merton Center at Bellarmine University in Louisville.

26. Louis Merton, "Wilderness and Paradise: Two Recent Books"; reprinted in Merton, *The Monastic Journey,* 144–50.

27. Merton to Erling Thumberg, December 15 and December 24, 1967, at the Thomas Merton Center at Bellarmine University in Louisville.

28. Merton, Working Notebook 28 (March–August 1967), n.p.

29. Merton, Working Notebook 32 (December 1967–May 1968) n.p. Merton's notes refer to Hugo Rahner, *Greek Myths and Christian Mystery,* trans. Brian Battershaw (New York: Harper and Row, 1963), xiv.

30. Merton, Working Notebook 34 (January–March 1968), n.p.

31. Merton, "The Wild Places," *Catholic Worker* (June 1968): 4, 6; "The Wild Places," *Center Magazine* (July 1968): 40–45; reprinted in Merton, *Thomas Merton: Preview of the Asian Journey,* 95–107.

32. Merton to Barbara Hubbard, December 23, 1967, and February 16, 1968, in *Witness to Freedom,* 72–75; see also *Thomas Merton: A Life in Letters,* 219–22.

33. Barbara Hubbard to Merton, November 28, 1967, at the Thomas Merton Center at Bellarmine University in Louisville. Hubbard, known as a futurist, social innovator, and author, has collaborated with Abraham Maslow, Jonas Salk, Lancelot Law Whyte, and Warren Wagar on evolutionary perspectives. Since 1992 she has been president of the Foundation for Conscious Evolution, whose vision statement has as its goal the "awakening of the spiritual, social, and scientific potential of humanity in harmony with nature for the highest good of all life."

34. Barbara Hubbard to Merton, February 12, 1968, at the Thomas Merton Studies Center at Bellarmine University in Louisville.

35. Weis, "Dancing with the Raven," 152.

36. Merton, Working Notebook 36 (May–October 1968), n.p.

37. Lane, *The Solace of Fierce Landscapes,* 76.

38. For more information on current activities of the Coalition on Environment and Jewish Life, go to www.coejl.org; for information on the World Council of Churches, go to http://fore.research.yale.edu/ religion/christianity/projects/wcc_jpc.html; the statement from the Philippine Catholic bishops can be found at www.aenet.org/haribon/bishops .htm; letters and encyclicals, as well as World Day of Peace addresses, can be found at www.vatican.va/edocs/ENG0214/_INDEX.HTM, www .vatican.va/holy-father/benedict_xvi/encyclicals/documents/hf _ben-xvi_enc_20090629_caritas-in-veritate_en.html; www.vatican. va/.../messages/peace/documents/hf_ben-xvi_mes_20091208_ xliii-world-day-peace_en.html.

39. Oliver, "The Summer Day," in *New and Selected Poems,* 94.

## Afterword

1. Kilcourse, " 'A Shy Wild Deer' "; Waldron, *Thomas Merton: Master of Attention,* 58.

2. Ehrlich, *The Solace of Open Spaces,* 62–64.

3. Ibid., 64.

4. Dillard, *Pilgrim at Tinker Creek,* 9.

5. Thoreau, *Walden,* 265.

6. Ruether, "Toward an Ecological-Feminist Theology of Nature," 147.

7. Prevallet, *In the Service of Life,* 16.

# Bibliography

Allchin, A. M. "The Worship of the Whole Creation: Merton and the Eastern Fathers." *Merton Annual* 5 (1992): 189–204.

Austin, Mary. *The Land of Little Rain*. 1903. Reprint, New York: Penguin Books, 1988.

Bate, Jonathan. *The Song of the Earth*. Cambridge: Harvard University Press, 2001.

Bernard of Clairvaux. *The Letters of St. Bernard of Clairvaux*. Translated by Bruno Scott James. Chicago: Henry Regnery, 1953.

Berry, Thomas. *The Dream of the Earth*. San Francisco: Sierra Club Books, 1988.

Blake, William. "Auguries of Innocence." In *Poetry and Prose of William Blake*, edited by David V. Erdman, 481–84. Garden City, N.Y.: Doubleday, 1970.

———. "The Marriage of Heaven and Hell." In *The Poetry and Prose of William Blake*, edited by David V. Erdman, 33–44. Garden City, N.Y.: Doubleday, 1970.

Burroughs, John. "The Art of Seeing Things." In *Leaf and Tendril*, 1–24. Boston: Houghton Mifflin, 1908.

Burton, Patricia A. *Merton: Vade Mecum*. Louisville: Thomas Merton Foundation, 1999.

Butigan, Ken. "Thomas Merton's Vision of the Natural World." In *Cry of the Environment: Rebuilding the Christian Creation Tradition*, edited by Philip N. Joranson and Ken Butigan, 337–46. Santa Fe: Bear and Co., 1984.

Byron, George Gordon. *The Poetical Works of Byron*, edited by Robert F. Gleckner. Boston: Houghton Mifflin, 1975.

Carson, Rachel. *Silent Spring*. 1962. Reprint, Boston: Houghton Mifflin, 1994.

———. *Silent Spring*. 40th anniversary ed. Boston: Houghton Mifflin, 2002.

Conway, J. North. *American Literacy: Fifty Books That Define Our Culture and Ourselves*. New York: William Morrow, 1993.

Cunningham, Lawrence S. "Thomas Merton: Firewatcher." *The Merton Seasonal* 15.2 (Spring 1990): 6–11.

Dillard, Annie. *Pilgrim at Tinker Creek*. 1974. Reprint, New York: HarperPerennial, 1998.

Ehrlich, Gretel. *The Solace of Open Spaces*. New York: Viking, 1985.

Elder, John. *Reading the Mountains of Home*. Cambridge: Harvard University Press, 1998.

Eliade, Mircea. *Patterns in Comparative Religion*, translated by Rosemary Sheed. New York: Sheed and Ward, 1958.

Emerson, Ralph Waldo. "Nature." In *Selections from Ralph Waldo Emerson*, edited by Stephen E. Whicher, 21–56. Boston: Houghton Mifflin, 1960.

Fox, Matthew. *The Coming of the Cosmic Christ*. New York: Harper and Row, 1988.

Grayston, Donald. *Thomas Merton: The Development of a Spiritual Theologian*. New York: Edwin Mellen Press, 1985.

———. *Thomas Merton's Rewritings: The Five Versions of* Seeds/New Seeds of Contemplation *as a Key to the Development of His Thought*. Lewiston, N.Y.: Edwin Mellen Press, 1989.

Greeley, Andrew. *The Catholic Imagination*. Berkeley: University of California Press, 2000.

Griffin, John Howard. *A Hidden Wholeness: The Visual World of Thomas Merton*. Boston: Houghton Mifflin, 1970.

Griffin, Susan. *Woman and Nature: The Roaring inside Her*. New York: Harper and Row, 1978.

Hamma, Robert M. *Landscapes of the Soul: A Spirituality of Place*. Notre Dame: Ave Maria Press, 1991.

Hart, Patrick. *Thomas Merton: First and Last Memories*. Bardstown, Ky.: Necessity Press, 1989.

Heinrich, Bernd. *Mind of the Raven: Investigations and Adventures with Wolf-Birds*. New York: Ecco, 1999.

———. *Ravens in Winter*. New York: Summit Books, 1989.

Hieb, Marianne. *Inner Journeying through Art-Journaling: Learning to See and Record Your Life as a Work of Art*. London: Jessica Kingsley, 2005.

Hopkins, Gerard Manley. *The Poems of Gerard Manley Hopkins*, 4th ed., edited by W. H. Gardner and N. H. MacKenzie. New York: Oxford University Press, 1988.

Jackson, Kenneth H. *Studies in Early Celtic Nature Poetry.* Cambridge: Cambridge University Press, 1935.

Jeffers, Robinson. "Letter to Sister Mary James Power" (October 1, 1934). In *The Wild God of the World: An Anthology of Robinson Jeffers,* edited by Albert Gelpi, 189–90. Stanford: Stanford University Press, 2003.

Johnson, Rochelle L. *Passions for Nature: Nineteenth-Century America's Aesthetics of Alienation.* Athens: University of Georgia Press, 2009.

Julian of Norwich. *Revelations of Divine Love.* New York: Penguin Classics, 1999.

Keats, John. *Selected Poems and Letters: John Keats,* edited by Douglas Bush. Boston: Houghton Mifflin, 1959.

Kilcourse, George A. "'A Shy Wild Deer': The 'True Self' in Thomas Merton's Poetry." *Merton Annual* 4 (1991): 97–109.

Kingsolver, Barbara. *Small Wonder.* New York: HarperCollins, 2002.

Kroll, Gary. "Ecology as a Subversive Subject." *Reflections* 9.2 (May 2002): 10–12.

Labrie, Ross. *Thomas Merton and the Inclusive Imagination.* Columbia: University of Missouri Press, 2001.

Lane, Belden C. *Landscapes of the Sacred: Geography and Narrative in American Spirituality.* New York: Paulist Press, 1988.

———. *The Solace of Fierce Landscapes: Exploring Desert and Mountain Spirituality.* New York: Oxford University Press, 1998.

Lear, Linda J. *Rachel Carson: Witness for Nature.* New York: Henry Holt, 1997.

———. "Rachel Carson's *Silent Spring.*" *Reflections* 9.2 (May 2002): 3–7.

Lentfoehr, Sister Thérèse. *Words and Silence: On the Poetry of Thomas Merton.* New York: New Directions, 1979.

Leopold, Aldo. *A Sand County Almanac.* New York: Oxford University Press, 1949.

Lipsey, Roger. *Angelic Mistakes: The Art of Thomas Merton.* Boston: New Seeds, 2006.

Lopez, Barry. "A Literature of Place." *Portland* (Summer 1997): 22–25.

Lyon, Thomas J. *This Incomparable Land: A Guide to American Nature Writing.* 1989. Reprint, Minneapolis: Milkweed, 2001.

Macquarrie, John. *Paths in Spirituality.* New York: Morehouse, 1993.

McDonagh, Sean. *To Care for the Earth: A Call to a New Theology.* London: Geoffrey Chapman, 1986.

McFague, Sallie. *The Body of God: An Ecological Theology.* Minneapolis: Fortress, 1993.

McKibben, Bill, ed. *American Earth: Environmental Writing since Thoreau.* New York: Library of America, 2008.

Merton, Ruth. *Tom's Book,* edited by Sheila Milton. Monterey, Ky.: Larkspur Press, 2005.

Merton, Thomas. "The Art of Poetry." Columbia University class notes, 1938. Friedsam Memorial Library, St. Bonaventure University, Olean, N.Y.

———. *The Asian Journal of Thomas Merton,* edited by Naomi Stone, Patrick Hart, and James Laughlin. New York: New Directions, 1973.

———. *Bread in the Wilderness.* New York: New Directions, 1953.

———. *Cold War Letters,* edited by Christine M. Bochen and William H. Shannon. Maryknoll, N.Y.: Orbis, 2006.

———. *The Collected Poems of Thomas Merton.* New York: New Directions, 1977.

———. *Conjectures of a Guilty Bystander.* Garden City, N.Y.: Doubleday, 1966.

———. *Contemplation in a World of Action.* Garden City, N.Y.: Doubleday, 1971.

———. *The Courage for Truth: The Letters of Thomas Merton to Writers,* edited by Christine M. Bochen. New York: Farrar, Straus and Giroux, 1993.

———. *Dancing in the Water of Life: Seeking Peace in the Hermitage. The Journals of Thomas Merton,* vol. 5, *1963–1965,* edited by Robert E. Daggy. San Francisco: HarperSanFrancisco, 1977.

———. *Day of a Stranger.* Salt Lake City: Gibbs M. Smith, 1981.

———. *Entering the Silence: Becoming a Monk and Writer. The Journals of Thomas Merton,* vol. 2, *1941–1952,* edited by Jonathan Montaldo. San Francisco: HarperSanFrancisco, 1996.

———, ed. *Gandhi on Non-Violence.* New York: New Directions, 1965.

———. *The Hidden Ground of Love: The Letters of Thomas Merton on Religious Experience and Social Concerns,* edited by William H. Shannon. New York: Farrar, Straus and Giroux, 1985.

———. *In the Dark before Dawn: New and Selected Poems of Thomas Merton,* edited by Lynn Szabo. New York: New Directions, 2005.

———. *The Inner Experience: Notes on Contemplation,* edited by William H. Shannon. San Francisco: HarperSanFrancisco, 2003.

———. *Learning to Love: Exploring Solitude and Freedom. The Journals of Thomas Merton,* vol. 6, *1966–1967,* edited by Christine M. Bochen. San Francisco: HarperSanFrancisco, 1997.

———. *Love and Living,* edited by Naomi Burton Stone and Brother Patrick Hart. New York: Farrar, Straus and Giroux, 1979.

———. *The Monastic Journey: Thomas Merton,* edited by Patrick Hart. Mission, Kans.: Sheed, Andrews and McMeel, 1977.

———. *New Seeds of Contemplation*. New York: New Directions, 1962.

———. *No Man Is an Island*. New York: Harcourt, Brace, Jovanovich, 1978.

———. Notebooks 10–43. Thomas Merton Center, Bellarmine University, Louisville, Ky.

———. *The Other Side of the Mountain: The End of the Journey. The Journals of Thomas Merton*, vol. 7, *1967–1968*, edited by Patrick Hart. San Francisco: HarperSanFrancisco, 1998.

———. *Passion for Peace: The Social Essays*, edited by William H. Shannon. New York: Crossroad, 1995.

———. *Raids on the Unspeakable*. New York: New Directions, 1966.

———. *The Road to Joy: The Letters of Thomas Merton to New and Old Friends*, edited by Robert E. Daggy. New York: Farrar, Straus and Giroux, 1989.

———. "The Root of War." *Catholic Worker* (October 1961): 1, 7–8.

———. "The Root of War Is Fear." In *New Seeds of Contemplation*, 112–22. New York: New Directions, 1961.

———. *Run to the Mountain: The Story of a Vocation. The Journals of Thomas Merton*, vol. 1, *1939–1941*, edited by Patrick Hart. San Francisco: HarperSanFrancisco, 1995.

———. *A Search for Solitude: Pursuing the Monk's True Life. The Journals of Thomas Merton*, vol. 3, *1952–1960*, edited by Lawrence S. Cunningham. San Francisco: HarperSanFrancisco, 1996.

———. *Seeds of Contemplation*. New York: New Directions, 1949.

———. *The Seven Storey Mountain*. New York: Harcourt, Brace, 1948.

———. *The Sign of Jonas*. New York: Harcourt, Brace, 1953.

———. *Thomas Merton: A Life in Letters*, edited by William H. Shannon and Christine M. Bochen. San Francisco: HarperCollins, 2008.

———. *Thomas Merton: Preview of the Asian Journey*, edited by Walter H. Capps. New York: Crossroad, 1989.

———. *Thoughts in Solitude*. New York: Farrar, Straus and Cudahy, 1958.

———. *Turning toward the World: The Pivotal Years. The Journals of Thomas Merton*, vol. 4, *1960–1963*, edited by Victor Kramer. San Francisco: HarperSanFrancisco, 1996.

———. "The Wild Places." *Catholic Worker* (June 1968): 4, 6; and *The Center Magazine* (July 1968): 40–45.

———. "Wilderness and Paradise: Two Recent Books" *Cistercian Studies* 2.1 (1967): 83–89.

———. *Witness to Freedom: The Letters of Thomas Merton in Times of Crisis*, edited by William H. Shannon. New York: Farrar, Straus and Giroux, 1994.

———. *Zen and the Birds of Appetite*. New York: New Directions: 1968.

Meyer, Kuno. *Selections from Ancient Irish Poetry*. 1911. Reprint, London: Constable, 1928.

Moffitt, John. "To Look at Any Thing." In *Reflections on a Gift of Watermelon Pickle,* edited by Stephen Dunning, Edward Lueders, and Hugh Smith. Glenville, Ill.: Scott, Foresman, 1966.

Mott, Michael. *The Seven Mountains of Thomas Merton*. Boston: Houghton Mifflin, 1984.

Muir, John. *My First Summer in the Sierra*. 1911. Reprint, New York: Penguin Books, 1987.

Nelson, Richard K. *Make Prayers to the Raven: A Koyukon View of the Northern Forest*. Chicago: University of Chicago Press, 1983.

Nepo, Mark. *The Book of Awakening*. San Francisco: Conari Press, 2000.

Nhat Hanh, Thích. *Peace Is Every Step: The Path of Mindfulness in Everyday Life*. New York: Bantam, 1991.

Northbourne, Lord (Walter James). *Religion in the Modern World,* 2nd rev. ed. Ghent, N.Y.: Sophia Perennis, 2002.

O'Collins, Gerald, SJ, and Edward G. Farrugia, SJ. *A Concise Dictionary of Theology*. New York: Paulist Press, 2000.

O'Donohue, John. "The Inner History of a Day." In *To Bless the Space between Us: A Book of Blessings*. New York: Doubleday, 2008.

O'Hara, Dennis Patrick. "'The Whole World . . . Has Appeared as a Transparent Manifestation of the Love of God': Portents of Merton as Eco-Theologian." *Merton Annual* 9 (1996): 90–117.

Oliver, Mary. "The Summer Day." In *New and Selected Poems,* 94. Boston: Beacon Press, 1992; originally in *House of Light*. Boston: Beacon Press, 1990.

Panikkar, Raimundo, ed. *Blessed Simplicity: The Monk as Universal Archetype*. New York: Seabury Press, 1982.

Pearson, Paul M. "The Ox Mountain Parable: An Introduction." *Merton Annual* 15 (2002): 14–19.

Plant, Judith. "Toward a New World: An Introduction." In *Healing the Wounds: The Promise of Ecofeminism,* edited by Judith Plant, 1–4. Philadelphia: New Society, 1989.

Prevallet, Elaine M., SL. *In the Service of Life: Widening and Deepening Religious Commitment*. Nerinx, Ky.: Loretto Earth Network, 2002.

Rilke, Rainer Maria. *Rilke's Book of Hours: Love Poems to God,* translated by Anita Barrows and Joanna Macy. New York: Riverhead Books, 1996.

Ruether, Rosemary Radford. "Toward an Ecological-Feminist Theology of Nature." In *Healing the Wounds: The Promise of Ecofeminism,* edited by Judith Plant, 145–50. Philadelphia: New Society, 1989.

Shannon, William H. *Something of a Rebel: Thomas Merton, His Life and Works*. Cincinnati: St. Anthony Messenger Press, 1997.

————. *Thomas Merton: An Introduction*. Cincinnati: St. Anthony Messenger Press, 2005.

Shannon, William H., Christine M. Bochen, and Patrick F. O'Connell. *The Thomas Merton Encyclopedia*. Maryknoll, N.Y.: Orbis Books, 2002.

Steindl-Rast, David. "Recollections of Thomas Merton's Last Days in the West." *Monastic Studies* 7 (1969): 1–10.

St. John, Donald. "Deep Geography: Nature and Place in *The Sign of Jonas*." *Merton Annual* 4 (1991): 39–58.

Thoreau, Henry David. *Walden* (1854), edited by Paul Lauter. New York: Houghton Mifflin, 2000.

Vreeland, Susan. *The Forest Lover*. New York: Penguin, 2004.

Waldron, Robert. *Thomas Merton: Master of Attention*. London: Darton, Longman, Todd, 2007.

Watson, Bruce. "Sounding the Alarm." *Smithsonian* (September 2002): 115–17.

Weil, Simone. *Waiting for God,* translated by Emma Craufurd. 1951. Reprint, New York: HarperCollins, 2001.

Weis, Monica, SSJ. "Beyond the Shadow and the Disguise: 'Spots of Time' in Thomas Merton's Spiritual Development." *The Merton Seasonal* 23.1 (Spring 1998): 21–27.

————. "The Birds Ask: 'Is It Time to Be?': Thomas Merton's Moments of Spiritual Awakening." In *Beyond the Shadow and the Disguise: Three Essays on Thomas Merton,* edited by Keith Griffin, 10–27. Holmfirth, West Yorkshire: Thomas Merton Society of Great Britain and Ireland, 2006.

————. "Dancing with the Raven: Thomas Merton's Evolving View of Nature." In *The Vision of Thomas Merton,* edited by Patrick F. O'Connell, 135–53. Notre Dame: Ave Maria Press, 2003.

————. "Dwelling in Eden: Thomas Merton's Return to Paradise." In *Riscritture dell'Eden,* edited by Andrea Mariani, 225–44. Rome: Liguori Editore, 2005.

————. "Kindred Spirits in Revelation and Revolution: Rachel Carson and Thomas Merton." *Merton Annual* 19 (2006): 128–41.

————. "Living Beings Call Us to Reflective Living: Mary Austin, Thomas Merton, and Contemporary Nature Writers." *The Merton Seasonal* 17.4 (Autumn 1992): 4–9.

————. "Merton's Fascination with Deer: A Graceful Symphony." *The Merton Journal: Journal of the Thomas Merton Society of Great Britain and Ireland* 15.2 (Advent 2008): 33–46.

————. "Merton's Poetry: Early Recognition." *The Merton Seasonal* 21.2 (Summer 1996): 8–11.

————. "Rambling with the Early Merton." *The Merton Seasonal* 28.2 (Summer 2003): 3–6.

―――. *Thomas Merton's Gethsemani: Landscapes of Paradise.* Lexington: University Press of Kentucky, 2005.

―――. "The Wilderness of Compassion: Nature's Influence on Thomas Merton." *Merton Annual* 14 (2001): 56–80.

Wheat, Jennifer. "Metamorphosis in Myth: Privilege or Punishment?" *Common Ground* 1.2 (2002): 10–18.

Williams, Terry Tempest. *Red: Passion and Patience in the Desert.* New York: Pantheon Books, 2001.

Wordsworth, William. *The Prelude: 1799, 1805, 1850,* edited by Jonathan Wordsworth, M. H. Abrams, and Stephen Gill. New York: W. W. Norton, 1979.

Worster, Donald. *Nature's Economy,* 2nd ed. Cambridge: Cambridge University Press, 1994.

# Permissions

The author wishes to thank the following publishers for permission to use excerpts from Thomas Merton's works:

"A Psalm" by Thomas Merton, from *The Collected Poems of Thomas Merton*. Copyright © 1949 by Our Lady of Gethsemani Monastery. Reprinted by permission of New Directions Publishing Corp.

"In Silence" by Thomas Merton, from *The Collected Poems of Thomas Merton*. Copyright © 1957 by the Abbey of Gethsemani. Reprinted by permission of New Directions Publishing Corp.

"Hagia Sophia"
"Love Winter When the Plant Says Nothing"
"Night-Flowering Cactus"
"O Sweet Irrational Worship"
By Thomas Merton, from *The Collected Poems of Thomas Merton*. Copyright © 1963 by the Abbey of Gethsemani. Reprinted by permission of New Directions Publishing Corp.

"Song for Nobody" by Thomas Merton, original by Cesar Vallejo, from *The Collected Poems of Thomas Merton*. Copyright © 1963 by the Abbey of Gethsemani. Reprinted by permission of New Directions Publishing Corp.

*Day of a Stranger* by Thomas Merton and edited by Robert E. Daggy, Peregrine Books. Copyright © 1981 by the Merton Legacy Trust. Reprinted by permission of the Merton Legacy Trust.

*Run to the Mountain: The Journals of Thomas Merton*, vol. 1, *1939–1941*, by

Thomas Merton and edited by Patrick Hart. Copyright © 1995 by the Merton Legacy Trust. Reprinted by permission of HarperCollins Publishers.

*Entering the Silence: The Journals of Thomas Merton,* vol. 2, *1941–1952,* by Thomas Merton and edited by Jonathan Montaldo. Copyright © 1995 by the Merton Legacy Trust. Reprinted by permission of HarperCollins Publishers.

*A Search for Solitude: The Journals of Thomas Merton,* vol. 3, *1952–1960,* by Thomas Merton and edited by Lawrence S. Cunningham. Copyright © 1996 by the Merton Legacy Trust. Reprinted by permission of HarperCollins Publishers.

*Turning Toward the World: The Journals of Thomas Merton,* vol. 4, *1960–1963,* by Thomas Merton and edited by Victor A. Kramer. Copyright © 1996 by the Merton Legacy Trust. Reprinted by permission of HarperCollins Publishers.

*Dancing in the Water of Life: The Journals of Thomas Merton,* vol. 5, *1963–1965,* by Thomas Merton and edited by Robert E. Daggy. Copyright © 1997 by the Merton Legacy Trust. Reprinted by permission of HarperCollins Publishers.

*Learning to Love: The Journals of Thomas Merton,* vol. 6, *1966–1967,* by Thomas Merton and edited by Christine Bochen. Copyright © 1997 by the Merton Legacy Trust. Reprinted by permission of HarperCollins Publishers.

*The Other Side of the Mountain: The Journals of Thomas Merton,* vol. 7, *1967–1968,* by Thomas Merton and edited by Patrick Hart. Copyright © 1998 by the Merton Legacy Trust. Reprinted by permission of HarperCollins Publishers.

# Index

CPSIA information can be obtained at www.ICGtesting.com
Printed in the USA
BVOW020917130112

280377BV00001B/3/P